THE
WATER GARDEN

THE
WATER GARDEN

ANTHONY PAUL · YVONNE REES

VIKING

VIKING
Viking Penguin Inc., 40 West 23rd Street, New York, New York 10010, U.S.A.
Penguin Books Canada Limited, 2801 John Street, Markham, Ontario, Canada L3R 1B4

First published in 1986 by Viking Penguin Inc. in simultaneous
hardcover and paperback editions

Published simultaneously in Canada

THE WATER GARDEN was conceived, edited, and designed by
Frances Lincoln Limited, Apollo Works, 5 Charlton Kings Road,
London NW5 2SB.

Library of Congress Cataloging in Publication Data
Paul, Anthony, 1945-
  The water garden.

  Includes index.
  1. Water gardens.   I. Rees, Yvonne.   II. Title.
SB423.P29   1986   635.9′674   85-40802
ISBN 0-670-81143-2

Printed in Yugoslavia by Mladinska knjiga, Ljubljana

Set in England by Chambers Wallace, London

CONTENTS

FOREWORD

Writing a book on a subject close to one's heart seems a fairly simple task at first. One of my greatest loves has always been water gardening. In fact, I am fascinated by water in the landscape and over the years I have enjoyed the challenge of introducing water into my designs for gardens. To me, its attraction and overall appeal is the way its slightest noise or movement can change the entire feeling of any space. So, to put pen to paper, organize my ideas and impressions of water and to call my first book *The Water Garden* seemed as easy as falling off a log. It wasn't long, however, before I realized that I required some professional help if the book was ever to get beyond the first scribbled notes. I was full of ideas of how to show my potential readers fascinating garden designs, adventurous swimming pools, sensual hot tubs and exotic waterfalls, but on the practical side there was text, there were methods of construction, there was maintenance, and there were many different factors that added up to producing a book that gave practical information as well as good design ideas.

It was at this stage that I contacted Yvonne Rees and begged her to become involved. Without Yvonne, with her editorial background and journalistic experience, this book could not have come into being, and I owe her a great deal for all the time, effort and energy she has put into the day-to-day aspects of translating my sometimes vague ideas into hard copy.

Water is so vital within the ecology of the world, and the environmental pressures on our seas, lakes, rivers and all watercourses have never been so heavy. Not just pressure from industry, but also from intensive agriculture, urban sprawl and rural misuse. Perhaps we all take for granted our early morning cup of tea or coffee, the water for which has been treated to provide fresh drinking water, but yesterday was possibly extracted from a flowing river. To keep our water clean and healthy we have to be aware of its very vital role in our lives and in the lives of plants.

This book, however, is not an environmental book, but, rather, it is intended to assist and help you to design with water as a flexible and very exciting medium. For those of you who already have a water garden, I would like to convince you to look at it again, become more aware of its importance and perhaps consider doing more with this natural asset. For those looking to build a water garden from scratch, I hope you will find some fascinating and helpful ideas and concepts that you may like to explore and adapt to your own particular garden. This may sound a little serious, but there is no reason why water in the garden shouldn't be fun, too. To this end, I have included plenty of designs and information on swimming pools, hot tubs, spas and splash pools.

Wildlife is without doubt one of the major attractions of water, and while I sit here at home in Surrey, England, looking out over a pond I made several years ago, I can see a beautiful kingfisher diving for minnows. For me, the presence of this bird is the greatest reward for all the hard work I have done in my water garden. Today it would be hard to imagine living where water was not a major part of my life.

In the back of this book you will find an acknowledgments section in which the people who have made substantial contributions to *The Water Garden* are credited. I must, however, single out Ron Sutherland for his exceptional help. His excellent photographs make an immense contribution to the final book.

Finally, Yvonne and I would like to thank everybody at Frances Lincoln Limited who made this book possible, and in particular Steven Wooster and Jonathan Hilton.

INTRODUCING THE WATER GARDEN

The development of the water garden to the present day; the advantages of water in your garden; the opportunity to grow exotic plants, attract a wide variety of wildlife, and simply enjoy the recreational aspects of water

WATER IS THE magic element that controls our lives even before we breathe air into our lungs. We live surrounded by water, and without it we cannot eat, drink or survive. Yet water has always been more than just an essential commodity – its great mystical and religious significance spans centuries and cultures. Most of us will recognize the sense of contentment a tranquil pool can inspire, or the feeling of awe when confronted by a roaring waterfall, and the appeal and power of water shows no signs of diminishing in our modern age. Wherever large prestigious buildings spring up, invariably they include some form of indoor or outdoor water feature in an attempt to add life and interest to an otherwise sterile urban environment. Health spas, too, are more popular than ever, and water is a strong determining factor in where we take our vacation: sailing, swimming, cruising or relaxing, by sea, lake, river or mountain stream.

The aim of this book is twofold: to inspire those garden lovers who feel that water could play a greater, more imaginative part in their lives, and to give practical help with the many possibilities water offers as a landscape feature in gardens, whatever their type or size.

– WATER GARDENS IN HISTORY –

It was logical that in climates of extreme heat, such as in the Middle and Far East, water should be appreciated for its cooling qualities. As the ancient civilizations that sprang up along rivers such as the Euphrates and the Nile prospered, pleasure gardens were built in which water, so vital for irrigation, became a major element in landscape design. In Ancient Egypt, as early as 1225 BC, Rameses III cultivated water lily ponds. It is known that the Incas of Peru were building gold and silver water channels, pools and basins from around 2500 BC. Water also became an essential element of the inner courtyard where weary travellers could rest, soothed by its sound, beside fresh, cooling pools and fountains. Inside the house, water ran in channels beneath the floor to provide a most effective cooling system.

ABOVE *The Alhambra makes extensive use of water to set off its exquisite Moorish architecture, with a series of beautiful formal courtyard pools designed to reflect the surrounding buildings.*

RIGHT *The setting of this Gothic-style house in Gloucestershire has all the familiar elements of a classic English country garden, softened by areas of water and a muted range of colored blooms.*

It was the Chinese, and later the Japanese, who perfected the water garden as imitation of the natural landscape. They looked to their gardens as a symbol of perfection and tranquillity representing the elements of heaven and earth and, from about the third century AD, had already established the pattern for the essential oriental garden, complete with island, lake and bridges. By the early fifteenth century they had turned it into an art form, exploring the sound, movement and energy of water. A reflective pool was the perfect symbol of earth meeting sky, and might represent a vast ocean, a river or a deep mountain lake, just as a series of boulders symbolized a mountain range or raked sand a desert.

The Japanese went further and developed the 'dry' garden: where water was not available, their designers cleverly used pebbles, sand, wood and rocks to represent a stream's course (see p. 10). Thus nature was recreated as a subject for contemplation, and this philosophy remains, refined but unaltered, in Japanese gardens today.

In medieval Europe, water was just making the transition from the purely functional to the recreational. The spring or well, still an essential source of water for the home, was often integrated with a formal garden and made the focal point of a circular or geometric design. In monasteries, the formal carp pool provided a valuable source of fresh food as well as a suitable spot for contemplation.

In Spain, the Moorish occupation led to the development of such famous courtyard gardens as the Alhambra with its fountains and canals. Here water was used to add vitality and sound to this lovely palace complex, which might otherwise have been a stark, rather forbidding building.

During the Renaissance, formal water gardens flourished as never before, especially in Italy where sculptural fountains became a fine art form, climaxing several centuries later with Bernini's

Monet's garden at Giverny was the inspiration for many of his paintings. Here he sought to capture the everchanging nature of light on water and the soft reflected colors of plants and flowers.

Oriental garden design
Japanese design shows a real feel for and under-standing of water (left). This understanding is emphasized in the dry water gardens below, where rocks or stones can be used to suggest a watercourse or stream, and raked gravel, pebbles and sand, the natural ripples of a pool.

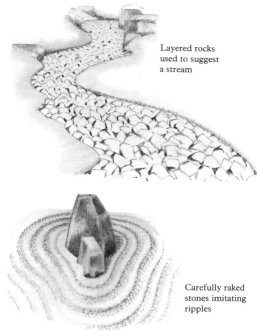

Layered rocks used to suggest a stream

Carefully raked stones imitating ripples

fabulous Baroque fountains, still very much in evidence in Rome's central piazzas. In the private gardens and estates, water was equally important, elaborate pools and waterfalls constructed in imitation of the Roman villa gardens designed so many years before.

At Louis XIV's seventeenth-century palace at Versailles outside Paris, the elaboration of water gardens reached a peak: watermills and pumps took water from the river Seine to operate 1400 fountains.

By the eighteenth century, the focus of water gardening had shifted to the English countryside and back toward a more naturalistic approach (see p. 8).

Following the Romantic movement in literature and painting, the Romantic landscape garden movement became very popular throughout the country. Huge lakes were excavated, streams built, valleys dammed and hillsides sculpted – preferably with the odd picturesque ruin perched on top.

Lancelot (Capability) Brown, whose name is synonymous with English landscape design, helped with the relandscaping of Chatsworth in Derbyshire – a classic English garden. It is famous for its fine water features, particularly the Great Water Staircase and Seahorse that survive from the earlier seventeenth century formal water garden.

Though few people today have the resources or would indeed want to copy the splendid if sometimes bizarre ideas of those who practiced water gardening in earlier centuries, the principles of using water shown by their talented gardeners and designers remain the same, whether applied to a grandiose design or to a tiny city garden. To design with water is the dream of many gardeners – it has more vitality and allows more flexibility than any other landscape medium – and by visiting or leafing through photographs of the great gardens created by earlier designers, we can absorb many ideas, some of which will seem startlingly fresh and innovative.

WHAT WATER HAS TO OFFER

◆

As some of the best garden designers over the centuries have demonstrated, water offers marvelous possibilities in both garden and landscape design. Its complete flexibility means that it can suit any type of garden and can even alter the shape of a site visually. A wide pool, for example, widthwise across a long garden will make the garden appear shorter, whereas a long, thin pool running down the length of the garden will make it appear longer. Visual tricks can be played with mirrors, too, and wooden decks can be used so they overlap the water's edge to give the impression that the water flows underneath.

If you want to make the most of a small area, the light-reflecting properties of water can be a great asset. The gleam of a pool adds an extra dimension and life to a garden, however small, and a stream or watercourse will give a shining ribbon of light by day or moonlight. Whether lit at night or not, most water features will look good, casting dramatic shadows.

Water doesn't just reflect light, of course, but like a soft-focus filter on a camera will reflect its surroundings (see right), blurring and magnifying colours

A pool's surroundings are vital for providing interesting reflections. Here, a formal pool is the perfect mirror for a modern house framed by trees and lush waterside plants.

ABOVE *Ducks prefer some kind of shelter built onto a raft in the middle of an expanse of water where they will be safe from predators.*

LEFT *Fish, such as these handsome koi carp, are part of the pleasure of owning a pool or pond. These sizable fish have become tame enough to be fed by hand.*

and shapes in an attractive approximation of the real world. Moving forms of surrounding trees, shrubs and marginal plants create an ever-changing pattern on the water's surface, highlighted by colors of leaves and flowering plants.

A moving water feature, such as a fountain, stream or waterfall, adds yet another dimension – or makes an excellent water design in its own right if you lack space for a pool or pond. As well as adding the visual excitement of white, or moving water, which sparkles and catches the light in a completely different way from still water, it produces sound – anything from gentle splashing to a roar, depending on the size and type of feature.

– CHOICE OF PLANTS –
Apart from the opportunities provided by a water feature itself, it allows the gardener to grow some wonderful plants.

Moisture-loving plants tend to be remarkable: not necessarily showy and bright, but giant-leaved and with striking forms and often delicate blooms. Because they rely on short growing seasons and high levels of moisture, they tend to have vigorous and fast-maturing habits. A small pool is worth installing simply for the chance to grow one or two lovely water lilies, an elegant bamboo or wonderfully lush ferns. If even a small pool is out of the question, a boggy, waterlogged area can still offer scope for planting some fascinating plants.

The cost of stocking a water garden is relatively low when compared with conventional planting. The use of one or more plants as the main theme of the planting is more usual and the plants themselves tend to grow faster because their roots are in water. The plants in general are easier to maintain and spread to cover the water's surface in a very short period of time.

– A PLACE FOR WILDLIFE –
A pleasurable bonus of having a pool or stream is that it provides a welcome home for a variety of wildlife. Apart from any fish that you may introduce, you will soon find it populated by creatures from tiny insects and dragonflies to birds, frogs, snakes, ducks and even small mammals who come to drink and sometimes stay to nest. The larger your pond and more natural its setting, the greater the variety and rarer the breed of visitor it will attract. In the garden featured on pp. 30-3, a beautiful kingfisher raids the pool near the house every evening and various small mammals, including mink, have been spotted in the undergrowth. In city locations, too, it is surprising what wildlife will be drawn to the area.

When a large multinational company built their new headquarters in London complete with outdoor water garden, it was not long before it had a thriving community of fish and ducks.

– WATER FOR FUN –

Ornamental water features satisfy our eyes and ears – and soothe our souls – but water can be for fun, too. Ideas for planning swimming pools, splash pools, hot tubs and spas into your water design have been included in this book because we believe that they are all part of water gardening, and add to our physical pleasure and enjoyment of water. Even a full-sized swimming pool can be designed so that it looks part of the existing garden landscape and not just an eye-catching, or rather eye-jolting, expanse of blue. In a small or exposed site, consider combining a swimming pool with an ornamental pool, or with other naturalistic features to help landscape it into the rest of the garden.

If you have no space for a swimming pool, then a splash pool, a heated spa with massage jets, or a separate hot tub near the house offer many of the advantages of a recreational water feature without the space and installation problems. They take up little room and will add a new dimension to barbecues and parties. If you do have the space – and money, too – why not combine them all in one 'leisure complex' complete with changing rooms, shower and eating area?

– ADVANTAGES OF A WATER GARDEN –

Once a pool or other water feature is installed, it matures quickly, creating an almost instant garden. Water-loving plants are prolific growers and will provide height, ground cover or dense screening in a single season. They are well worth all the time and effort spent at the planning stages when you realize just how little effort they require once established.

Because a pool or pond is a fairly self-contained environment, water gardens also avoid many of the growing difficulties associated with soil type of the conventional garden. Though cooler climates still affect the range of tender plants that you can grow, the use of soil backfilling on waterside shelves, or containers for water plants both in and out of the water, or on pool surrounds, means that you have more control over the growing medium which can be easily adjusted to suit a particular plant's preferences.

Water gardens are generally easier to maintain, too, especially when pools are combined with paving or wooden-decked areas with tubs of plants rather than grass, thus avoiding constant mowing, edging and feeding. Because so many water plants have vigorous growing habits, you should have little trouble with weeds, which tend to get choked out by foliage as the growing season advances.

Despite their striking and often impressive results, you don't have to be a professional landscape architect to tackle the majority of the ideas and designs suggested in this book. Large pools will need the help of professional equipment and a machine operator for excavation, but most of the construction techniques utilize a few basic skills and a lot of hard work rather than special knowledge or tools.

A well-landscaped lagoon-style pool like this example is great fun to use and does not spoil the design of the rest of the garden.

– A Natural Setting –

Anyone who has seen a water meadow in full flower with its orchids, *Mimulus,* forget-me-nots and marsh marigolds, an alpine stream tumbling down a rocky ravine, or a clear chalk creek bubbling over pebbles, will understand the desire to recreate such lovely features in their own garden. It is possible to capture the atmosphere and appearance of a natural stream, waterfall or pool if you observe closely how they are created in the landscape, how the position of rock or soil influences its shape and if you keep strictly to natural materials in your construction: stones and boulders, seasoned lumbers, logs, shingle, pebbles or gravel.

Naturalistic water gardens, whether Romantic, oriental-style, or with a meadow or woodland setting, are easier to plan and construct than their more formal counterparts, such as the formal geometric pools and canals of the Alhambra (see p. 8) or Hampton Court near London. Yet, interestingly, you will find that even a formal pool has an almost wild, natural feel simply because water plants tend to have such random habit and informal shape.

As a general rule, however, a pool in a natural water garden should have an informal, irregular shape that fits well with the contours of your site, with its edges concealed by stones, boulders or plants. Alternatively, the pool could have a graduated depth with water lapping at a sloping beach of pebbles or shingle. Adding a bog garden between a pool and another part of the garden, or installed as a feature in its own right, helps create an excellent wild atmosphere and as a marginal area will encourage a wider variety of wildlife. It blends easily into most settings and is simple to construct, requiring no great work of excavation and no restriction of its shape or size. For a romantic feel, again, the more ambitious water gardener may like to design a stream winding through a course of boulders or a rocky waterfall tumbling into a small, rock-edged pool.

All these ideas for natural water gardens are developed in the chapters that follow, incorporating formal as well as informal features, for both small and large gardens. If, as we hope, they encourage you to include some form of water feature in your own garden, you will see for yourself why water holds such fascination and offers so much pleasure.

ABOVE *This small natural stream is almost hidden by wild, water-loving plants growing along its banks and in the long grass of the meadow beyond, providing excellent cover for wildlife.*

LEFT *The naturalistic waterfall blends into the backdrop of trees and dense green plants thanks to a careful arrangement of rocks and boulders planted with ferns, which cling to the crevices.*

CHOOSING A WATER FEATURE

Selecting and adapting a suitable water feature for your particular needs; types of water feature for both small and large gardens; a detailed look at how eight established city and country water gardens were designed, constructed and planted

A GARDEN THAT is totally unsuitable for any kind of water feature would be a rarity indeed, but you must also bear in mind that practical limitations are only overcome at an increased cost of installation and maintenance. The photographs in this book should give you a good idea of the type of feature suitable for your site, but other considerations apply, such as whether you have reasonable access, if you intend excavating a pool or pond using a mechanical digger. Bear in mind that you must allow a clear run for machines to maneuver around the site and to clear away spoil, and this may be restricted by an already developed garden.

– SUITABILITY OF YOUR GARDEN –

Soil and subsoil type rarely present a problem when constructing a water feature unless you are trying to sink a pool into solid rock substrata or the site has a high water table (the level at which water drains to naturally). In both these cases, a raised pool is advised to avoid difficulties. As far as growing water plants is concerned, with artificial pools soil type is easily adapted to suit any plants that are at all fussy since the pool and its edges are an enclosed environment and soil has to be introduced anyway, or the plants grown in pots and baskets. The only soil problem you are likely to encounter is on a free-draining gravel or sandy site where you want to create a natural stream or pool without any synthetic linings. Your only option here is to 'clay puddle' the bottom using imported natural clay (see p. 131).

Climate will of course restrict the variety of water or waterside plants that you can grow, and in colder climates the more tender ones will have to be

removed to the shelter of a frost-free greenhouse during the winter months.

Water features in extremely hot regions will be troubled by high evaporation levels, particularly in small shallow features, with water supply problems at certain times of year. You should only install a feature if you can guarantee enough water to sustain both it and plant and animal life all year round. There are ways to help overcome this problem, such as creating dappled shade with trees and pergolas, and avoiding having any moving water features, such as fountains and waterfalls, which have a higher-than-normal evaporation rate.

The best place to site your water feature is probably the first thing you

Raised pools are ideal for difficult terrain or for disabled gardeners, but their edges may need careful screening with evergreen shrubs and beds or containers of attractive plants.

need to know, and there are a few recommendations and restrictions worth noting. The ideal site is sheltered from prevailing winds by evergreen trees or shrubs, or screens, is easily accessible for both installation and maintenance work such as cleaning, is reasonably close to electrical facilities – if you are considering installing lighting or if your feature will require the operation of a pump – and is close to drainage facilities. It should also receive plenty of sunshine – the warmer the water, the greater the variety of plants available.

Pools and most deciduous trees are not happy companions (see pp. 119-21 for recommended pool-side trees) unless you are prepared to net the pool in autumn or spend time raking out dead leaves before they pollute the water. With large, natural lakes the problem is not so acute, since the volume of water and the organisms living in the water aid the decomposition of vegetable matter. But a small pond or family swimming pool should definitely be situated away from any large deciduous trees or shrubs.

It is also not a good idea to site a pool too close to a neighbor's wall or fence if this makes either access or landscaping difficult.

Apart from these practical considerations, try to position your water feature where it will have most effect. A pool or stream hidden at the bottom of the garden, even if intended as the finale of a design, tends to be neglected and forgotten. Conversely, water always looks good close to the house where its reflective quality combined with that of the windows makes an interesting play of light, especially at night when the building is lit up.

It is also enjoyable to view a pool or other water feature from the house, particularly when the weather is cold, or, better still, to be able to open patio doors or French windows directly onto it. Most formal pools or other small water features work very well in conjunction with a well-designed patio, and add life and movement to a sometimes dull area.

When considering the positioning of a swimming pool, hot tub or spa, proximity

An indoor water feature can encompass all the charm of a natural pool without the climatic limitations. Here, massed plants flourish in a heated conservatory setting.

Safety in the water garden
Water features need special thought if there are young children in the household. Pools of any depth are too dangerous, but a small fountain or waterspout draining into a concealed reservoir makes a stylish water feature. Alternatively, a trickle of water over a pebbly stream, like the one shown below, is safe enough to play in and can be drained quickly at the touch of a switch if you are called away.

to the house is particularly important for convenience of use. Unless you have the means and space to build a changing room, shower and bar/kitchen complex adjoining your pool, you will be reluctant to make a long walk across a large garden carrying food, drinks and equipment.

– WHAT SIZE FEATURE? –

As big as you can conveniently afford seems to be the rule that applies to ponds and pools in the garden, since water maximizes the effects of its surroundings, as described earlier and as some of the photographs on the following pages show. This rule does not necessarily apply to moving water features such as waterfalls which, if very large, can be extremely difficult to operate successfully (see p. 60). In general, though, gardeners tend to err on the small side, losing a small feature in the undergrowth of a large garden or installing a preformed pool unimaginatively because they did not think they had the space or money for anything more ambitious. You will be wasting your money, however, if your water feature ends up looking boring and insignificant, simply because you could not think of a better or cheaper way of installing it, or could not wait until you could afford to have the job done properly. Yet there are ways you can reduce the expense without economizing on size, quality or style, for example by using second-hand materials. Excavation of a large pond or pool is always going to be expensive, however, and the only way to cut costs is either to do the job yourself or to offer your services as a laborer to someone who knows what they are doing. Pool linings cannot be economized on either, since they must be of the best quality, whether concrete, butyl or PVC, but it often pays to shop around and try to get a better price. Calculations should always be checked and double checked, since mistakes are expensive to rectify.

When it comes to stocking a water feature with plants, bear in mind that good quality, healthy water plants can quickly add up to a tremendous price if you are stocking a feature all in one go. But remember that most water plants are vigorous growers and will rapidly spread to cover an area and can therefore be introduced sparingly. For this reason also, it makes sense to set up an exchange system with family and friends so that cuttings and root stocks can be obtained for free, and you need not then let the cost of planting out a pond put you off increasing its size at the planning stages.

There are no hard and fast rules about restricting your planting designs either: giant-leaved species can look magnificent used with discretion next to a small water feature; or smaller, more modest species can create wonderful effects planted in single massed groups around a lake.

– TRYING OUT IDEAS –

Given the great scope and flexibility for designing water features in the garden, it can be difficult to know where to start. Begin by drawing a scale map of your garden on graph paper, plotting in any permanent features such as buildings, boundaries, hedges, trees and shrubs. You can then experiment by mapping in different types of water feature to see how they might look in purely design terms. When you have something you think might work, transfer it to the garden itself by tracing the outline of the shape of your proposed feature onto the ground using a length of hose or string. View it from as many angles as you can, not forgetting from inside the house. A completely empty, featureless site will be entirely open to your imagination, but with most sites there will usually be some aspect or existing feature to start you off, such as a naturally damp hollow, or a stream or former stream bed. Or, the contours of the ground in your garden might suggest an informal shape for a free-form swimming pool, thus helping it to blend in with its surroundings. A rockery is always a good starting point for a waterfall combined with a pond or stream at its base; a change of level or sharply sloping site will lend itself to cascades, or a series of linked pools.

FEATURES FOR SMALL GARDENS

Even the smallest town garden, back-yard or balcony can benefit from the creative use of water. Because of its light-reflecting and magnifying qualities, water in the smallest pond will maximize the effect of plants and other features around it. A tiny trickle fountain, an old ceramic sink with miniature water lilies, or an old-fashioned faucet set in a wall and producing a steady trickle into a tiny pool or pretty bowl will add life to a dull patio area. In shady corners where there is insufficient light to support plant life, you might have water trickling down sheets of clear glass or fiberglass, or down thin copper rods in a simple but very effective modern-style waterfall.

For small gardens with a little more scope and sunshine, water can be combined with other features such as a modest rockery with a waterfall, and delicate alpine plants alongside the more dramatic water ones. Or, in a formal patio garden, build a combined feature of raised pool and planting beds.

Inexpensive, improvised pools can be attractive and unusual despite their limitations of size and design, perhaps planted with a single beautiful water lily such as *Nymphaea pygmaea alba*, N. 'Graziolla', or N. 'Froebeli'. Old sinks can be roughened with a coating of glue size and exterior textured paint, or use a

ABOVE *A length of bamboo spouting water into a large oriental urn and its surround of glistening pebbles make a small but harmonious arrangement, offering the sight and sound of water in a very limited space.*

RIGHT *This old stone trough looks perfectly at home in a meadow of long grass and wild flowers and provides a constantly changing view of plants and sky reflected in the still surface of the water.*

Water adapts well to a relatively small garden, where an ambitiously large pool area simply serves to make the garden appear larger than it really is.

stone trough, wooden barrel or even a large hollowed-out log. A deep, raised stone trough with a water lily and a few fish can make a lovely eye-level feature within a formal seating area for the elderly or disabled, surrounded by raised beds of sweet-smelling herbs and flowers. Barrels, on the other hand, look best sunk in the ground, with smooth stones or pebbles placed round the rim.

Some of the more formal water features are particularly well-suited to small patio areas where they stand out and where their effect can be closely controlled. If you don't have the space for a pool and fountain, a handsome mask that spouts water into a bowl (see p. 62) or a bubble fountain (see p. 132) can be a most satisfying and effective alternative.

A small formal pool based on a rigid geometric shape is, in fact, a surprisingly flexible starting point for creative design. A square or rectangular pool, planted with a single clump of reeds, or other specimen plant, perhaps at the foot of a stone statue, produces a clear mirror effect. A more ambitious design might have a series of small, similar-shaped pools linked to create patterns, or positioned on different levels, and planted with a limited but complementary selection of water plants.

Other small water features can take advantage of the particular site. Sloping ground can be used to create a cascade tumbling through a series of weirs to a pool at its lower level, or a permanently damp area can be turned into a bog

garden. Many of the plants that will grow well in naturally poorly drained or continuously wet areas are superb for the beauty of their flowers and for their architectural form – plants such as irises, primulas and marsh marigolds, or the spectacular large-leaved skunk cabbage. Artificially made bog gardens are cheaper and easier to install than ponds, and can even be contained in an old sunken barrel or old stone sink with its plug-hole used for ready drainage.

The more ambitious small-garden owner may be tempted by photographs on the pages that follow to try something rather more daring and dramatic. Incorporating a large water feature into a small garden takes some nerve and means considerable upheaval during its installation, but the result often transforms the area into a tranquil retreat which belies its urban surroundings. For the really brave, with a suitable sunny site, it is possible to convert the whole area into one continuous water feature with low wooden walks and wooden deck patio areas for eating and sunbathing. The advantages of such a garden are particularly attractive to those who don't much care for gardening or who have very demanding jobs as, apart from being easy to maintain, a garden with much of its area given over to water will provide a very unurban environment.

An expanse of water will make a small garden look much bigger than it really is and, together with clever planting, will distract the eye from its true boundaries, while irregular pond shapes help disguise the shape of the site altogether.

Even formal pools look good surrounded by the soft greens, yellows, pinks and mauves of waterside plants and more wild-garden flowers.

This moatlike curve of water effectively divides off part of the garden. It has been edged in brick and stone to match the retaining wall and creates a circular paved seating area.

Apart from using mirrors to double a pool's size, or overlapping a pond's edge with timber or stone slabs so that the water appears to continue beneath, there are other 'tricks' for making a water feature look bigger. Tall, dramatic planting using shrubs and trees on the far bank will always make a small stretch of water more imposing. Using gravel or small pebbles to construct a graduated beach into the water has the effect of making the water appear deeper, too.

Unless you are prepared to let it take over your whole garden, a full-sized swimming pool is usually considered to be out of the question for small gardens (though they can sometimes be landscaped sympathetically – see p. 52). But small garden owners need not be totally deprived of the pleasures of a recreational water feature; splash pools take up very little space and provide a cooling diversion for adults and children in hot weather, and can be fitted with optional massage jets. Even more compact and easier to install because they remain above ground are hot tubs, which can be used all year round.

Mirrors set into a false brick arch create the impression that the water flows through the wall and beyond. This type of trompe l'oeil *makes the garden look much bigger than it really is.*

FEATURES FOR LARGE GARDENS

Deciding on a water feature for a large garden is in many ways more difficult than for a small one. If a pond is not to look insignificant, you have to scale up your ideas and think big. When designing the feature, construction details must be considered most carefully both from a practical and a financial point of view. It may be better to plan several separate but interconnected features than one enormous one, not only because this will look more interesting, but also because the water garden can then be tackled in various stages, perhaps over a period of years, as time and budget permit.

Any large expanse of water such as a small lake, a large pond or even a wide stream will be more interesting if interrupted, or broken up, by devices such as fountains or small islands, sitting areas or crossing points. Bridges and stepping stones should always serve a decorative as well as a functional purpose – which does not mean to say that they should be fussy or elaborate.

A large feature is also more likely to be viewed from many different angles, and this must be taken into consideration at the planning stages – not forgetting the middle of the water if you are building bridges and stepping stones.

Fountains and water sculptures are an excellent eye-catching way of breaking

Large informal water features need an impressive backdrop of trees and shrubs to provide scale, shelter and interesting reflections. Quick-growing waterside plants are useful for softening the banks and lilies help to break up the surface.

up the water area, equally suitable for formal and informal water features. They can be very simple (see pp. 61-3) but they must be of sufficient size not to be dwarfed by their immediate surroundings – perhaps a single tall plume of water showering onto the otherwise still surface of a lake.

Most people would regard a lake or large pond as an informal feature, its edges blurred by large groups of reeds, grasses and other waterside plants. This is certainly most attractive and is ideally suited to large, often rural gardens where woodland walks, areas of rough grass and natural planting surround the water area. However, there is no reason not to create

a large water feature with a formal atmosphere if that would be more in keeping with the style of your house and garden. While a fully enclosed geometric pool or series of pools in the classical style with rows of statues and balustrading would be prohibitively expensive for most people, some stone balustrades, a statue or two and a large formal fountain combined with more restrained planting can create the right sort of effect. Even a natural lake in a formally laid out garden can look magnificent if it is linked to the rest of the garden by well-manicured lawns or paths.

For a totally different look, consider borrowing from the Japanese principle

of a complete miniature landscape design incorporating water, boulders, Japanese maples and stone bridges.

Wide streams or watercourses can be used effectively in large gardens, either to exploit the whole extent of a site or to divide it up into different areas accessible by bridges. A formal canal, long and perfectly straight, built of stone or brick, and culminating in a formal pool area can look splendid in a large garden, yet it is easy to maintain if the plants are restricted to pots and tubs along its sides.

Islands built on large ponds and lakes, and accessible by simple wooden bridges, create new vantage points to view the water and are perfect places for planting small trees and large plants.

A large sloping or rocky site naturally suggests a major waterfall or cascade feature, which could be combined with a stream or pool; alternatively, use the soil excavated from a pond to provide the height for such a feature.

A large garden also offers the opportunity for an ambitious bog garden, either adjoining a main pool, where it can simply form the damp edges of a natural lake, or contained within a brick or concrete border around the perimeter of a formal pool. A bog garden lends itself particularly well to having water running through it – the flow should be no greater than a steady trickle – and can make a pleasing feature at the end of an artificial stream, or where water can be diverted to run through a naturally low-lying part of the garden. Interest and access can be provided with stepping stones or wooden walks.

Numerous waterside plants grow well in a large bog garden; their root systems also help keep the water clean and act as a binding agent, preventing the soil being washed away. Be sure to cover as much of the area as possible with plants to prevent weed growth, and arrange large stones on any unplanted areas to reduce evaporation – this will provide a change of texture and will look more interesting, too. Large plants will need staking or anchoring with stones until their roots take hold. Avoid particularly invasive species such as forget-me-nots, some types of reeds, rushes and irises, unless your area is very large. Many ferns will thrive there too. Although you can't keep fish in a bog garden, the area will attract an interesting variety of wildlife.

A bog garden combined with a large pond offers even more scope for wildlife as together they provide cover and pro-

The area surrounding a naturalistic pond can be ideal for creating a bog garden, where a wide variety of plants will thrive in the damp, waterlogged soil.

tection. Encourage wildfowl and small mammals by growing plants such as *Typha, Acorus, Cyperus, Petasites* and bamboos which are ideal for nesting. If you want to encourage frogs and newts, a sloping sided pond will be more appreciated. No pool is complete, of course, without a few fish darting about and there is a guide to selecting and keeping different varieties on pp. 146-7. For outdoor pools, don't choose breeds that are too well camouflaged or you will never see them; lighter, gold-colored fish are the easiest to spot – although they are then more vulnerable to predators.

In large gardens there is more scope to integrate swimming pools with ornamental pools, but this combination needs careful planning. They may be linked by a small garden of lush water plants, or form part of a single design where the ornamental feature helps soften the often hard, uncompromising lines of the swimming pool.

ORIENTAL DECKED GARDEN

Low maintenance and a love of the oriental style were the twin inspirations for this garden, measuring 25m/82ft by 10m/33ft, centered round a semiformal water feature. The original garden was little better than a wilderness of rubble and brambles after nearly twenty years of neglect, and only a couple of yuccas and two beautiful firethorns (*Pyracantha*) were considered worth keeping and integrating into the revised plan.

The present owners are a busy working couple, so the new layout was designed to avoid lawns or flower beds that would require regular tending. The resulting combination of water, pebbles and wooden decks not only has a suitably Eastern 'feel', but it is easy to maintain and provides a flexible garden with areas for both relaxing and entertaining.

The pond is an interestingly irregular wedge shape spanning the width of the plot (to give the impression of breadth), and is framed by pine decks at varying levels. The supporting joists were rescued from the house when it was being modernized and are, therefore, well-seasoned and very suitable for the job. The butyl liner of the pool has been tucked under the deck, making the water appear as if it goes all the way underneath. On the other side, the water runs under a diagonally placed wooden bridge

THE PLAN

A suburban rectangular plot was given a new, far more interesting emphasis by using wooden decks to break up its length. The design carefully avoids any long, straight lines and creates a natural focal point in a light-reflecting stretch of water complete with a shallow pebble beach.

1 *Pyracantha* 'Orange Charmer'
2 *Vitis vinifera*
3 *Arundinaria japonica*
4 *Fatsia japonica*
5 *Ligularia* 'Othello'
6 *Carrygana arborescens*
7 *Sorbus vilmoriana*
8 *Betula pendula* 'Purpurea'
9 *Caltha polypetala*
10 *Ligularia clivorum* 'Desdemona'
11 *Sasa palmata*
12 *Rheum palmatum* 'Rubrum'
13 *Prunus* 'Shirofugen'
14 Mixed pot plants
15 *Yucca filamentosa*
16 *Miscanthus sacchariflorus*
17 *Ligustrum ovalifolium* 'Aureum'
18 *Philadelphus* 'Belle Etoile'

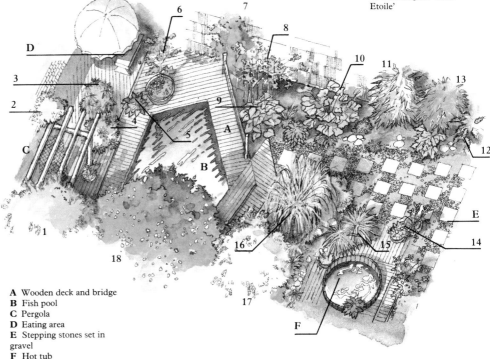

A Wooden deck and bridge
B Fish pool
C Pergola
D Eating area
E Stepping stones set in gravel
F Hot tub

and laps at a shallow pebble beach planted with clusters of flowering *Hosta lancifolia*.

The soil excavated to make the pond has been used to create a mound at one end, which adds an interesting change of perspective, as well as providing the opportunity to install running water in the form of a waterfall; a pump and filter are used to circulate clean pond water to the top of the mound.

In a Japanese-influenced garden, plant shape and form are as important as color and texture, and here the presence of water provides the perfect chance to grow water lilies, bold moisture-loving plants and a green mixture of ferns, ivies and mosses. An oriental-style garden

Viewed from the first floor of the house, the semiformal plan of the garden is revealed, with an irregular-shaped pond cleverly breaking up the length of the plot.

must, of course, have bamboo, and here various types have been planted in square areas filled with pebbles and sunk into the decks and in pots close by. Included is the more unusual *Sasa palmata* with long, hand-shaped leaves, which has been planted on the mound.

For added height, and to distract the eye from neighboring houses and gardens, a careful selection of trees for small gardens has been planted. These include the lovely, free-flowering Japanese cherry (*Prunus* 'Shirofugen'), which has late, longlasting blooms and the Swedish birch (*Betula pendula* 'Dalecarlica') with graceful drooping branches and deeply cut,

long, pointed leaves. There is no leaf-fall problem with this birch, and eventually it will hang down over the bridge in true Japanese fashion.

Flowers have been chosen for their subtle shades and shapes as well as the blooms themselves; plants such as the buttery yellow *Trollius* 'Golden Queen', which has been planted at the water's edge, and those excellent planting companions astilbes, with soft, pink fluffy flowers, and the purple hostas.

To break up the basic design of the garden and to soften the effect of the wooden decks, a fine contrast of different leaf shapes and colors has been

planted in gaps left between the planks and in large pots. Some of these are old pots rescued from the original garden. Other pots used come from Italy, China and the Far East and form part of a collection lovingly built up over the years. The owners tend to treat them like furniture, moving them around the garden to create a variety of effects. Apart from the pots and strong planting design, there are many other small touches to reinforce the oriental atmosphere, including the thick bamboo poles, which serve as simple railings along the bridge, the tall bamboo flares and the inexpensive reed mats used to screen unsightly walls and to provide an excellent disguise for an ugly shed too useful to demolish.

Bridge and decks have been deliberately designed so that one can walk round the garden, not straight up and down it. To strengthen this use of the garden, there are several seating areas at different points, placed to capture maximum sunshine during the day. Elsewhere, two separate wooden-decked terraces, one shaded by a wooden pergola, are provided with seating perfectly in keeping with overall design of the garden.

It is the combination of simple materials, such as wood, pottery, reed screening and smooth pebbles, around the central calm expanse of water, reflecting plants and sky, that gives this garden its relaxing atmosphere. The koi carp in the pond are tame enough to feed by hand and they now have a new neighbor – a mallard duck, which made its home by the water in the first year the pond was installed.

Because of their orientation, wooden decks round the pool area away from the house provide the ideal place to sunbathe, eat and entertain. Tubs of plants soften and enhance the atmosphere.

SOFTENING EDGES

A better overall effect is usually created if you can establish a theme for your garden and use plants and other features to disguise any construction elements. In this view (right) bamboo poles, reed mats and large stones encourage an oriental feel. Lush plantings of *Caltha polypetala* help to soften any hard lines produced by the edges of the bridge. *Caltha polypetala* has again been used (below), along with *Trollius europaeus* and *Ligularia* 'Desdemona', to help to naturalize a gently sloping pebble beach; while a lovely *Miscanthus sacchariflorus* (center) makes a fine, bushy specimen at the water's edge. The contrasting shapes of *Yucca filamentosa* and the broad leaves of *Rodgersia tabularis* make excellent planting companions, softening the area between wood and pebbles (below right).

SEMIWILD WATER GARDEN

Water is the dominating feature in this two-acre garden, with two large lakes almost dwarfing the pretty black and white house. The atmosphere today is wild and informal – sweeps of rough grass, woodland paths, wild flowers and rustic wooden bridges crossing tranquil stretches of water – but is a very different picture from when the present owners moved in a few years ago. Then it was more of a wilderness – completely untended and a tangle of undergrowth.

The new owners were keen to preserve the garden's air of seclusion and, despite its size, it had to be easy to maintain. Frequent business trips abroad left little time for tending beds and ornamental lawns and so an emphasis on water was ideal. To start, both lakes were dredged and cleaned and any established water-loving plants found in the tangle were split and moved to positions where their shape and color could be seen to best advantage. Spiky reeds and bulrushes were regrouped along the banks to form patterns of different shades of green. There are no flower beds as such, just dense clumps of large-leaved plants at the water's edge and spilling over onto the grass. More water-loving plants have been introduced over the years to provide year-round variety and color and, particularly in spring, the garden glows with yellow flowers of *Trollius*, *Caltha* and iris, bright against the dark-brown remains of last year's growth. In summer, large groups of water lilies (*Nymphaea* 'Gladstoniana') spectacularly dominate the water with huge leaves and enormous creamy-white flowers with golden centers. And to provide a cheering bright reflection in late summer and autumn, there are large clumps of *Ligularia clivorum* planted along the banks.

Surrounding the house and lakes is mostly mature woodland carpeted with rough grass studded with wild flowers, such as pink campion, English bluebells, primroses and English cowslips. Its natural appearance makes the perfect backdrop for the large informal ponds.

To form a link with the luxuriant plants around the water, lush and abundant groupings of plants have been added – magnificent prickly rhubarb (*Gunnera manicata*), a hardy native of Chile, and the rare black Chinese bamboo grown alongside the umbrella bamboo. Around the house, terracotta pots of all shapes and sizes have been planted with ferns and palms, creating a moist, watery effect, with sweet-smelling culinary herbs adding their gentle color and foliage to soften any hard contours.

LEFT *The stream feeding the lakes meanders through well-established clumps of hostas and* Hydrangea macrophylla.

RIGHT *A variety of waterside plants, reeds and bamboos leads the eye to the house and the backdrop of mature trees beyond, creating an enclosed, intimate atmosphere.*

THE PLAN

This large country garden, over several acres in size, had two established but overgrown lakes, one either side of the driveway. They were dug out and replanted and a new pool area created in an existing boggy site beyond the second lake. The lakes are fed by a natural stream that runs along one of the property boundaries; the lakes overflow one into another and then into land drains, which carry away any excess water. Wooden decks have been used to link the house to the water area by means of a jetty, which was extended to include seating and barbecue areas and a hot tub. Simple wooden bridges cross the water at various points, allowing the garden to be viewed from many angles. The planting design includes dramatic, broad-leaved specimens designed to suit the scale of the garden and to emphasize the natural country atmosphere of the setting.

1 *Peltiphyllum peltatum*
2 *Rheum palmatum*
3 *Miscanthus sinensis zebrinus*
4 *Ligularia* 'Gregynog Gold'
5 *Salix babylonica*
6 *Malus* 'Profusion'
7 *Hosta fortunei*
8 *Trollius europaeus*
9 *Caltha palustris*
10 *Primula japonica*
11 *Osmunda regalis*
12 *Scirpus*
13 *Nymphaea alba*
14 *Nuphar*
15 *Sorbus aria*
16 *Quercus robur*
17 *Salix purpurea* 'Pendula'
18 *Caltha polypetala*
19 *Miscanthus sacchariflorus*
20 *Iris pseudacorus*
21 *Alnus cordata*
22 *Heracleum mantegazzianum*
23 *Ligularia clivorum* 'Desdemona'
24 *Pinus sylvestris*
25 *Arundinaria japonica*
26 *Typha latifolia*

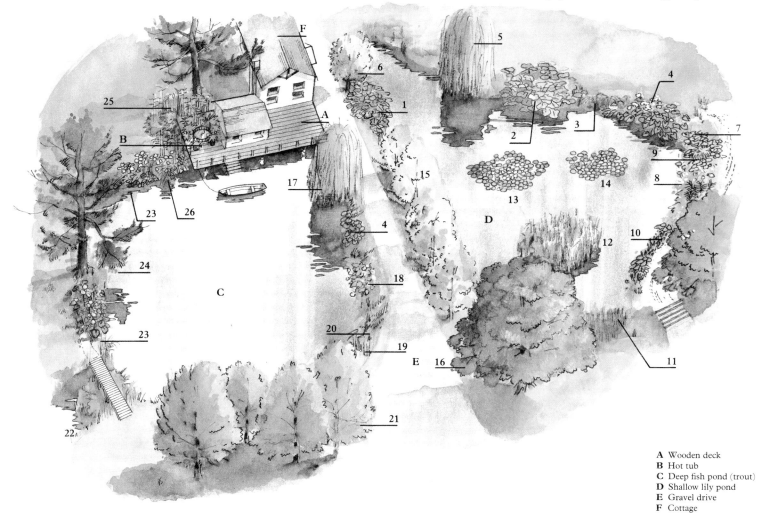

A Wooden deck
B Hot tub
C Deep fish pond (trout)
D Shallow lily pond
E Gravel drive
F Cottage

LEFT *Large areas of the shoreline surrounding the lakes have been naturalized. This not only provides a lush screen but also cuts down considerably on the amount of upkeep and maintenance required. The dappled shade provided by mature trees is appreciated by the ferns, which have now established large colonies and need periodic thinning to keep them under control.*

BELOW *Viewed from across the water of one of the lakes, the old timbered house is dwarfed by trees and plants. The lake itself has been planted with large, informal groups of foliage plants to provide a fascinating blend of leaf shapes and a patchwork of different shades of green.*

The exclusive use of seasoned wood for features such as bridges, walks and decks helps to maintain the country atmosphere and harmonizes well with the exposed outer beams of the old house. A wooden deck has been built out from the house to overlap the edge of the water, giving the impression that it runs right up to the building, and provides the perfect link between the house and water. Simple railings make this the obvious place to pause and stare out over the water's surface, and the deck does double duty as a jetty, with a simple wooden step down to a small canoe. The deck continues round the corner of the house with several changes of level to incorporate other areas of interest: two seating and eating areas (one at either side to catch maximum sunlight), a barbecue and, in a corner overlooking the water, a hot tub set into the deck and sheltered by a well-planted wooden pergola. It is a complete outdoor living complex, softened by tubs and baskets of plants designed to complement the lake and garden, especially at night when it is lit by spotlights.

Simple wooden bridges have been used to cross the water in several places, providing not only a series of focal points but also useful access to the opposite bank, encouraging a number of circuitous routes across the water and round the garden. Some wooden-planked bridges rest just above the water's surface and lead to two islands, which have now become naturally populated by colonies of moorhens.

LAGOON & SPA

A large sunny site may seem like a most desirable asset in a garden, but when it is steeply sloping and you are keen to install some form of swimming pool and patio area, it can present real problems. The family who own this hillside garden in Australia were beginning to despair when a local garden designer suggested they complement the surrounding land-

THE PLAN

The swimming pool and spa were built into a difficult sloping site by cutting into the hillside and building a concrete retaining wall. This wall has been faced with local slate, as has the area surrounding the pool and spa, which has been enlarged to provide level areas for eating, entertaining and sunbathing.

A Terracotta-paved steps
B Natural slate paving
C Eating area
D River pebbles and rocks
E Lagoon-style swimming pool
F Spa and jacuzzi

1 *Cyathea australis*
2 *Eucalyptus gunnii*
3 *Syzygium paniculatum*
4 *Blechnum nudum*

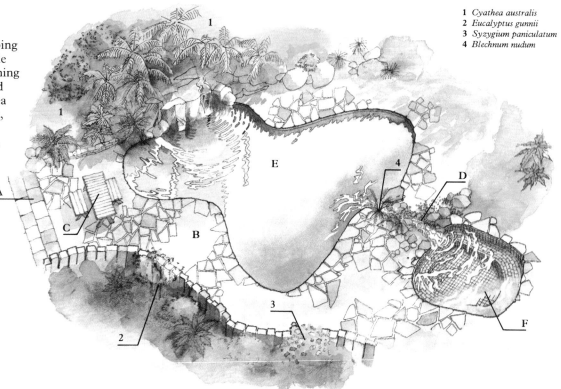

scape by combining a natural lagoon-type pool with a rocky waterfall.

The first job was to cut into the hill and build a concrete retaining wall imitating the natural contours of the hill. This was faced with rough slabs of local slate naturalized with tree ferns planted in the cracks and crevices. The pool itself was designed in an irregular shape, widening toward one end to imitate a

LEFT AND BELOW *A lagoon-style swimming pool with a natural-looking waterfall linked to a fully equipped spa was the perfect solution for this sloping garden site.*

natural lagoon and then lined with concrete set with tiny brown pebbles, which further help to soften its appearance. The area surrounding the pool has been paved with the same material used for the retaining wall and waterfall.

Set into the paving and adjoining the main pool is a small tiled spa, equipped with turbocharged booster pumps for maximum water agitation. The spa, complete with integral seating, has been lined with small, creamy-green tiles, and it is linked directly to the main pool by a little creek cut through the slate sur-

round. A shallow trickle of water runs over a layer of pebbles (like those of the main pool) set in the bed of the creek, with arrangements of larger rocks and feathery ferns, and physically links the two features.

The site around the water complex has been heavily planted with established gum trees to provide a lovely scenic backdrop and provide a more private, secluded environment. The trees' graceful foliage is mirrored in the jade green water of the pool and is balanced by lush plantings of native shrubs.

FORMAL POOL

The designer/architect of this garden in Belgium was presented with a tricky problem: how to hide a swimming pool in a perfectly level site with no natural relief or large distinguishing features. The rectangular pool had already been installed and the remainder of the garden laid to grass.

It was an ambitious project since the garden is large, with a traditional detached house and a family who all wanted to use the garden for their own particular needs. The solution was to convert the whole area into a water garden complex, incorporating the existing pool and providing other areas for eating, strolling and sunbathing. Although the new ornamental pool areas surrounding the swimming pool are almost formal in shape, the overall impression from the house and various vantage points round the site is one of a continuous stretch of water broken only by wooden-decked paths, patio-type platform areas and bold groups of foliage plants.

Taking the existing rectangular swimming pool as the starting point for the plan, it has been semienclosed by an almost U-shaped ornamental pool, linked

OPPOSITE *The house looks out over an extensive water garden with distinct plant groupings and linked by deck areas for sunbathing, eating and entertaining.*

THE PLAN

To disguise a full-size swimming pool in a large, level site, it has been integrated into a complete leisure and ornamental pool complex. The swimming pool has been surrounded on three sides by a semiformal ornamental pool, and the areas between them covered with wooden decks or thickly planted with waterside plants to create the impression that the water area is continuous.

1 *Gleditsia* 'Sunburst'
2 *Arundinaria japonica*
3 *Miscanthus sacchariflorus*
4 *Hemerocallis* 'Bonanza'
5 *Cortaderia argentea*
6 *Lysimachia punctata*
7 *Iris sibirica*
8 *Ligularia* 'Othello'
9 *Pontederia cordata*
10 *Nymphaea alba*
11 *Miscanthus sinensis gracillimus*
12 *Lythrum salicaria*
13 *Betula nigra*
14 *Verbascum nigrum*
15 *Miscanthus sinensis zebrinus*
16 *Geum rivale*
17 *Gynerium argenteum*
18 *Butomus umbellatus*
19 *Ligularia* 'Gregynog Gold'
20 *Monarda* 'Croft Way Pink'
21 *Ligularia przewalskii*
22 *Thalictrum aquilegiifolium*
23 *Lysimachia clethroides*
24 *Alchemilla mollis*
25 *Iris germanica*
26 *Arundinaria murielae*
27 *Ligularia clivorum* 'Desdemona'

A Wooden decks
B Reconstituted stone slabs
C Swimming pool
D Ornamental pool

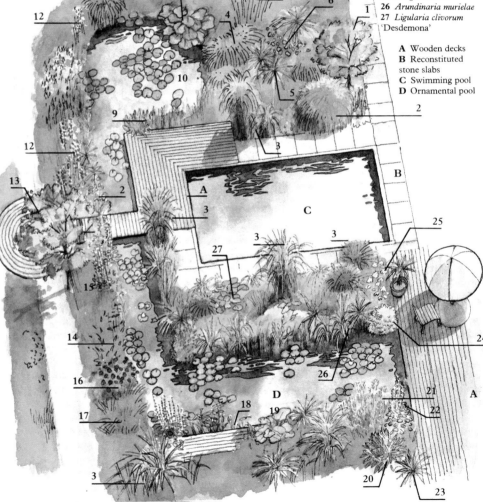

and crossed by areas of seasoned timber decks to make it look as though the water area is continuous. With lush planting along the water margins, this not only has the advantage of integrating and disguising the more functional pool, but adds to the pleasure of swimming in it.

The wooden-decked areas and walks are designed so as to complement both the formal and the ornamental pools, with the well-seasoned lumber providing a sympathetic and relatively unobtrusive surface that is safe and pleasant to walk on. They deliberately do not go through the center of the garden but, instead, provide a series of routes round, across and between the pools, encouraging leisurely strolls and close observation of the plants and other features.

Also integrated into the design are larger wooden platform areas, sheltered by clumps of vigorous water plants, with fine views of both water features. These platforms are used for separate sunbathing, dining and entertaining areas and are scattered round the site so that they can be used by different members of the family without causing any disturbance or annoyance.

Planting has been carefully controlled, with groups of aquatic and waterside plants dense enough to provide a screen and disguise the pool sides, but without spoiling the general shape and design of the garden. Large single-plant groupings, such as spiky *Miscanthus sacchariflorus,* loosestrife (*Lythrum salicaria*) and the flowering rush (*Butomus umbellatus*) help to soften the edges of the wooden deck and to trace interesting designs through the garden, reinforcing the impression that the water area is continuous. Small water lily colonies also add variety to the surface of the ornamental pool. A mixture of shape and form is provided by the different green foliage of spiky and broad-leaved plants, and soft-colored flowers are used to maintain a very tranquil, natural atmosphere. There are no giant-leaved or very tall specimens in this garden, since this would interrupt the overall view and upset what is a delicate blend of impressions designed to be easy on the eye. As an extension of this planting design, and to add an element of flexibility, more lush green foliage plants have been grown in terracotta pots, which are stood on the decks, in the water and close to the house, where they can be moved around or replaced as and when required.

Wooden decks used to segregate different areas of the water garden and set close to the water's surface allow the attractive water-loving plants to be seen at comfortably close quarters and their lovely variety of subtle colors to be appreciated from many angles.

CANAL-STYLE GARDEN

It may seem unusual to find a small water garden with a Chinese influence in the center of London, but this charming garden in Regents Park is perfectly in keeping with its nearby prestigious surroundings. The house and garden are behind the famous Nash Terrace and the house was once owned by Charles Dickens – he is believed to have written *Great Expectations* here. But the water feature and the oriental theme of the garden were inspired by the Regents Park Canal and the nearby lovely Chinese Pavilion.

The owners of the house are an architect and a designer, both with strong ideas on the form and style they wanted for their small city garden; they were keen to incorporate some acknowledgment of the influence the historic buildings in Regents Park had had on them. The site's restrictive size – only 20m/65ft long by 10m/33ft wide – was no discouragement for an ambitious and fairly elaborate design, including a wide stretch of water, strong structural features and, despite being heavily overshadowed by trees, a bold planting plan.

The starting point for the whole project was the Chinese-inspired pavilion/tea-house (based on the design in Regents Park) and constructed of seasoned wood at the farthest end of the

THE PLAN

A long, narrow site has been visually widened by dividing the garden in half with a water feature. The water spans the width and is reflected in mirrored arches either side. The water can only be crossed by means of a Chinese-style bridge and, on the farthest bank, a pavilion doubles as a summerhouse and an ornamental feature. Because the garden is heavily shaded by trees, planting in the water is restricted to shade-tolerant plants, such as reeds and lilies, and to bold waterside plants both in the water and in large tubs positioned round the garden.

1 *Arundinaria japonica*
2 *Prunus laurocerasus*
3 *Phyllostachys aureosulcata*
4 *Acer negundo*
5 *Mahonia japonica*
6 *Tilia cordata*
7 *Rodgersia pinnata*
8 *Rhododendron* 'Humming Bird'
9 *Skimmia japonica*
10 *Fatsia japonica*
11 *Acer palmatum*
12 *Vinca minor*
13 *Hedera colchica*
14 *Prunus*
15 *Nymphaea alba*
16 Mixed flowering annuals
17 *Acer japonicum*
18 *Fatshedera lizei*

19 Mixed annuals, rose, busy Lizzies
20 *Malus* 'Red Jade'
21 *Bergenia* 'Silberlicht'
22 Mixed potted shrubs
23 *Cornus controversa*

A Chinese pagoda
B Bridge
C Fish pool
D Fountain
E Mirror under arch
F Patio sitting area
G Steps to basement

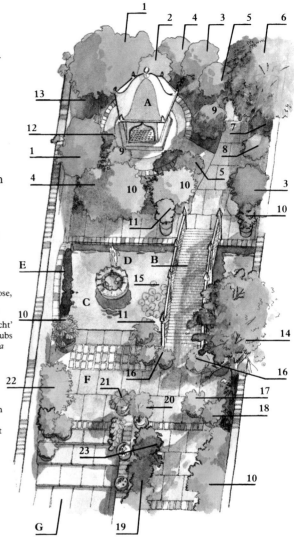

long, thin site. It makes a lovely ornamental feature, as well as being entirely practical, and is surrounded by bamboo, *Fatsia* and *Mahonia japonica*. The strong form and shape of this planting makes a fine evergreen backdrop against a thick curtain of large-leaved ivies grown to smother the steep walls defining the garden boundaries. Water has been used to divide this area from the rest of the garden and house, effectively cutting the garden in half; by spanning it across its width (from wall to wall), it makes the far end accessible only by means of an elegant wooden bridge. The bridge is of a beautiful Chinese design and stained an

LEFT *A stretch of water reminiscent of the nearby Regents Park Canal divides the garden in half, and is crossed by a Chinese-style bridge designed to match the pavilion at the far end. A miniature red rose adds a splash of color among the various shades of green.*

RIGHT *Seen from the pavilion, the water garden appears densely planted with dramatic moisture-loving plants, which soften the edge of the water and screen part of the bridge.*

attractive shade of soft Ming blue to match the pavilion.

The stretch of water is about 3m/10ft wide and runs from two mellow-brick arches built into the high walls on either side of the garden. These have been fitted with mirrors to give the impression that the water runs right through and continues either side, creating a feeling of continuity and space as well as bouncing light back onto the water. This effect is heightened at night, when the water's spotlit reflection appears to travel through the walls. Also reflected is a simple plume of water coming from a fountain in the middle of the water area. This relatively low-level feature tumbles into a scalloped stone bowl planted with water-loving plants and reflected in the arches, making it appear as if there is a whole series of them along the watercourse. As an added feature, the water has been stocked with plenty of goldfish, which seem to be thriving, and which can be observed from the pool sides and the bridge, set quite close to the water's surface.

The narrowness of the plot, the high walls and a spreading lime tree combine to make this a difficult garden to plant successfully. Although the dappled light effect is very pleasant on the water, most water plants need plenty of sunshine to make them flourish, and so here plants in the water have been restricted mainly

to reeds and the half-hardy arum lily (*Zantedeschia aethiopica*). Planting in the rest of the garden has been carefully chosen to create a strong, architectural look, with plants specially selected for their shade-tolerance and their affinity to water. These include big-leaved ivies to soften the walls and wooden structures and to provide ground cover; the large-leaved *Fatsia japonica*; *Miscanthus sacchariflorus*, a tall grass native to China; broad-leaved bamboos, such as *Sasa palmata*; *Rodgersia tabularis*, which conveniently prefers the shade of a tree close

to the water's edge and has beautiful round leaves and fluffy red flowers; and *Mahonia japonica*. Most of these plants have a definite oriental or Chinese feel about them, helping to set the atmosphere for the pavilion and Chinese bridge, and reinforced by rich, glazed Chinese pots placed round the garden. These have been planted with Japanese maples, bamboos, *Fatsia japonica*, the weeping crabapple and ornamental dwarf pines for a good variety of oriental-style foliage and forms. These are all dramatic yet tough plants, capable of withstanding the inevitable neglect of a busy working family and the pollution of a midcity location.

As well as the extensive use of seasoned wood, water and dense planting to soften the overall effect, warm stone and brick to match the high walls have been used to provide a well-defined edge to the pool and to create paths leading to the water's edge on both sides of the bridge. This is enhanced by the use of large river pebbles placed round the plants, in pots and continued into the water to create a softer, more natural, streamlike effect. The paving not only looks attractive but it is entirely practicable here where the garden is frequently used at night – it provides a safe, dry surface for guests unfamiliar with the layout of the garden. This is when the architectural features, such as the Chinese pavilion and bridge, come into their own, too, both elegantly lit when the garden is used at night for entertaining and providing an ideal place to sit and linger. These, and the dramatic planting combined with the natural draw of the water, tend to encourage people out into the air to investigate.

ABOVE *Brick arches built into the walls either end of the pool are fitted with mirrors to give the impression that the water runs through – an effect that is highlighted at night when the water's surface is lit.*

FAR LEFT *Natural stained wood for the bridge, a mellow brick wall and flowering* Vinca, *combine to create a very tranquil, natural stream effect.*

LEFT *Chinese-glazed pots of white miniature roses and the shiny green leaves of* Bergenia *'Silberlicht' are stood on the mature brick paths and edges at the waterside.*

TRANQUIL CITY GARDEN

This beautifully planted water garden in Holland is really quite modest in size – only 600sq m/718sq yd – yet it provides the perfect retreat for a city dweller who would really rather be living in the country. In fact, the house was bought with the garden firmly in mind: it is con-siderably larger than any other in the neighborhood, where the average size of plot is only about 60sq m/72sq yd. It also lies on the edge of the city, and so, once the surrounding houses were cleverly screened with trees and tall shrubs, the rest of the garden could be landscaped to blend with the country-side beyond to give the impression of greater space.

The owner of this garden is for most of the day confined to an office and there-fore wanted a garden that could be enjoyed easily when he came home. He liked the idea of creating a water feature, finding the tranquil effect of still water and succulent, moisture-loving plants very relaxing, and he also realized the low-maintenance advantages of such a feature. His other priority requirement was total privacy, and here again the dramatic, architectural form of water-side plants and their general rapid growth rate made them ideal for providing dense yet attractive screens. The original plan called for extremely close, tall planting indeed, not just to screen the garden from other houses, but also from passers-by using a proposed public pathway running adjacent to the garden's bound-aries. Luckily, plans for the pathway were later abandoned and so today the background of trees and shrubs does not have to be quite as massed.

The water feature itself has been designed as a large, formal L-shaped pool

THE PLAN

The corner of a modern house with floor-to-ceiling glass doors provides the pivot for this water garden fea-ture. The L-shaped pool has been designed to surround the building on two sides, linked by a narrow wooden deck. Dense planting is intended to lead the eye away from the house and toward the backdrop of large trees and shrubs. This has been graded down to clumps of waterside plants along the bank of the pool. Tubs of plants have also been used to soften the decked area close to the house and to link it with the rest of the garden.

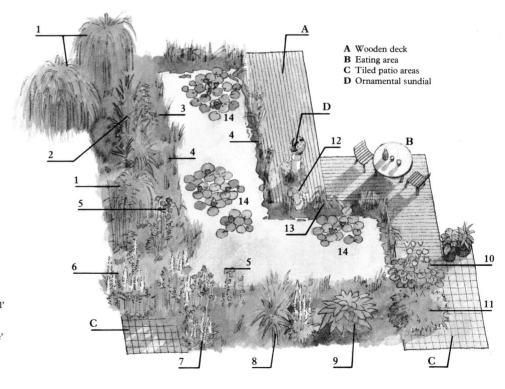

1 *Miscanthus sacchariflorus*	8 *Cimicifuga racemosa*
2 *Arundinaria japonica*	9 *Hosta sieboldiana*
3 *Butomus umbellatus*	10 *Ligularia* 'Othello'
4 *Pontederia cordata*	11 *Hemerocallis* 'Taj Mahal'
5 *Astilbe*	12 *Alchemilla mollis*
6 *Lysimachia punctata*	13 *Iris pseudacorus*
7 *Thalictrum flavum*	14 *Nymphaea* 'Escarboucle'

A Wooden deck
B Eating area
C Tiled patio areas
D Ornamental sundial

LEFT *Planting around this formal pool relieves any hard edges and forms a tranquil patchwork of shapes and colors on all levels.*

RIGHT *A wooden deck links house to water with a narrow platform overlooking the pool. Plants growing on the deck and indoors echo the foliage on the opposite bank.*

area framing two sides of the house, and it is the focal point for the whole garden. Lush planting along its banks and stretching to the farthest limits of the garden provides a bold, natural framework and concentrates attention on the gleam of the water, which bounces light and reflections through the floor-to-ceiling glass doors along both sides of the house. A narrow walkway of seasoned timber has been built right up to the house wall and overhangs the water, making it appear as if it flows under the building. It is one of the great pleasures of this house design that the doors of both the living and dining rooms can be opened to give direct access to the garden, making it possible to enjoy the water and its surrounding plants only 1.5m/5ft away – a great boon when entertaining during the summer months.

In order to encourage a feeling of continuity both inside and outside, the wooden deck has been set at exactly the same level as the interior floor and complements it in terms of warmth and texture, with large tubs of leafy plants positioned indoors and on the deck near the water's edge.

Along the edges of the pool nearest the house, low reeds, ornamental grasses and other waterside plants have been introduced to soften the horizontal lines of the deck, but without obscuring any view of the garden. The surface of the water is kept fairly clear of plants for the same reason, with a few irregular clumps only of small water lilies for summer color and to add interest to the area through the scattered disk effect produced by their padlike leaves. On the far bank, denser planting begins to build up with an interesting variety of size, shape and color: thick clumps of the yellow-flowering *Ligularia* and the quick-to-naturalize, spiky purple loosestrife (*Lythrum*), both of which attract bees and butterflies in summer when their flowers are in full bloom. But the flowers are really only a bonus, since the plants have been chosen more for their foliage, with the intention of creating a blend of tall spiky and broad-leaved species and a combination of different shades of green rather than a multitude of flower color. Beyond these, and providing a denser framework of foliage, is a well-thought-out selection of mature shrubs and trees. The gradation from house and pool to the trees just visible beyond the limits of the site is so subtle that one gets no impression at all of the garden's boundaries.

LARGE NATURAL GARDEN

An existing water meadow, divided from the garden by a rustic railed fence, sparked off the inspiration for this water garden and lake adjoining an old English farmhouse. In its original form, the garden was an unsightly area of rough grass and boggy patches, thick with clumps of rushes and sedges, while to the rear of the water meadow lay a natural stream meandering through a thicket of willows and elders. This group of trees suggested a far more sensible place to define the limits of the garden and, considering the damp, boggy conditions of the intervening land, it seemed natural to create a lake and water feature there.

This new area was designed to provide a vista at the end of the lawns, which run down toward it from the house, and the completed lake seems as if it has always been part of the farm's history.

The first step was to remove the soil to create a shallow lake bed, which was to be fed by the stream at the far end. This was achieved by pumping water from the

ABOVE RIGHT *Lawns and gardens lead down from the farmhouse to the new lake, where large clumps of waterside plants produce a very natural setting.*

RIGHT *The large surface area of the water is perfect for huge, irregular clumps of water lilies* (Nymphaea alba). *Reflected in the water is an everchanging pattern of light and shadow produced by the sky and surrounding trees.*

THE PLAN

A natural stream and a large water meadow at the end of the garden suggested the ideal site to create an informal pond feature to complement a traditional English farmhouse. The pond was dug out and the soil removed, rather than used for extensive relandscaping, which would have altered the existing views.

Recent additions to the design are islands for fishing and for wildfowl to nest, a bridge for access and a wooden jetty so that the pond can be used for boating. The pond has also been linked to the swimming pool (see p. 48), by means of a pleasant walk through bold, moisture-loving plants.

stream; water is returned back to the stream by means of an overflow, crossed by a bridge, to complete the system. The pump that feeds the lake also diverts water over a small waterfall made of rustic logs to create a fun water feature. Some of the soil from the excavation has been reused in the area round the fall to build gentle mounds and help to landscape it into the rest of the garden.

Over the years since its creation, the lake has been further enhanced by the addition of two islands with small bridges to connect them to the shore. These are used as places to sit and fish, to feed the ducks and for water fowl to use as nesting areas. In fact, since the lake and the surrounding plants have matured, it has become a popular place for a wide range of water fowl, and the lake has recently been stocked with trout, which seem to be doing well.

1 *Salix alba*
2 Dwarf mixed conifers
3 *Peltiphyllum peltatum*
4 *Rheum palmatum*
5 *Hosta fortunei*
6 *Nymphaea* 'Gladstoniana'
7 *Lysimachia clethroides*
8 *Alnus cordata*
9 Mixed *Azalea* hybrids
10 Mixed *Erica* hybrids
11 *Petasites japonicus*
12 Mixed *Rhododendron* and *Azalea* species
13 *Iris sibirica*
14 *Ligularia clivorum* 'Desdemona'
15 *Gunnera manicata*
16 *Pinus sylvestris*
17 *Caltha palustris* and *Pontederia cordata*
18 *Hosta fortunei*
19 *Iris pseudacorus*
20 *Arundinaria nitida*
21 *Salix babylonica*
22 Hedge of mixed shrubs
23 *Gunnera scabra*
24 *Typha latifolia*
25 *Scirpus albescens*
26 *Calla palustris*
27 *Nymphaea alba*

A Lake
B Waterfall feeding lake
C Jetty
D Steps to lawn and house
E Bridge to island
F Stream
G Outlet and overflow

A small waterfall and pool made of rustic logs adds movement and interest to the garden and also conceals the pump that feeds the new lake from the stream.

Providing a wonderful framework for the water is a mass of dense foliage – a combination of water-loving shrubs and plants that have grown vigorously in the moist, rich conditions. Plants such as hostas, *Ligularia, Peltiphyllum,* azaleas, magnolias and *Cornus* create a mass of colorful form and shape, offering something eye-catching throughout the year. To add to the pleasure of the water area, a small landing jetty has been constructed from seasoned lumber, and a simple canoe allows the family to view the shorline and its plants from any-on the lake surface and to tend to the deeper planted water lilies.

Having plenty of land to spare and a love of water in all its forms, this family was also keen to build a swimming pool somewhere in the garden. Their main concerns were that it should be as sensitively placed and landscaped as their ornamental water feature and that the two be linked in some way, not necessarily directly but to suggest some common bond between them. The solution was a low-lying water garden between the two and running parallel to the existing stream. While the lake and the swimming pool are perfectly separate entities, they are reached by a walk through large-leaved waterside plants and exotic bamboos, which help establish the watery nature of the two areas. The swimming pool itself is completely hidden by an old barn and well screened for privacy and protection from prevailing winds by solid plantings, trellis, wood and brickwork, all of which help it to blend with the traditional style of the house and nearby barn.

The pool is an irregular kidney shape designed to create a more natural contour and it is surrounded by mellow-colored paving similar to weathered terracotta. Beyond this is a dense arrangement of evergreen shrubs and small trees providing not only a screen but a wide variety of leaf shape and color.

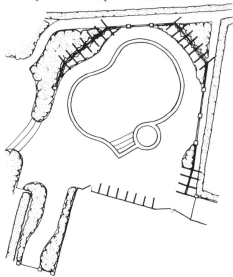

The swimming pool is concealed and sheltered by a wide variety of evergreen shrubs and trees, and it is reached from the main pond area through a small connecting garden.

Bold waterside plants, reeds, wild grasses and native flowers ring the pond and merge naturally into the closer-cropped lawns beyond.

BOLD LEAF SHAPES

This large, informal water garden relies on dramatic planting patterns to create maximum effect. In the view right, *Hosta* 'Thomas Hogg', fringing a grassy path, has a striking yellow-edged, deep green leaves. When you have large spaces to fill, the giant *Rheum palmatum* (far right) is a good choice, dwarfing as it does surrounding foliage with its enormous, fringed leaves. For smaller areas, however, *Ligularia clivorum* 'Desdemona' and *Iris pseudacorus* (below) provide an interesting contrast of leaf shape beside the water. In the moist conditions of a large water garden, an almost junglelike profusion of waterside plants will flourish. In the photograph (right) large-leaved *Petasites japonicus, Hosta sieboldiana* and the feathery fern *Dryopteris filix-mas* mingle different shapes and shades of green in the dappled light beneath mature trees.

NATURAL SWIMMING POOL

The owners of this Australian garden have two young teenage children and so a full-size pool and heated spa were important. But they also wanted a garden they could enjoy looking at, where they could entertain friends and which was in keeping with their house – a fine Victorian building with an elegant veranda opening directly onto the garden. The difficulties with this site lay in the fact that the garden was small and very level, which meant that the pool was bound to dominate. The solution proved to be to make a feature of it, using natural materials and informal shapes to play down the more functional aspects of the swimming pool.

The pool is a softly curving, free-form shape designed to fit the site exactly, with plenty of room for back-planting and paved seating areas near the house. Although the site is small, access was not difficult via the driveway, making the removal of excavated soil and rubble relatively easy. The immediate pool surround is of old, convict-made bricks, which is a practical surface to keep clean yet mellow enough not to make the pool look brand new.

The large heated spa has been cleverly integrated into the pool design, tucked into one of the curves nearest the house and tiled to match the blue of the pool. Enough old bricks were tracked down from demolished buildings (and buffed by sandblasting to bring out their colors) to surround the spa, too, making a pleasant patio area adjoining the house. This leads naturally onto the veranda itself, which has stout wooden piers and full-length glass doors opening onto the family room and kitchen. The latter has a

The large informal sweep of the swimming pool is surrounded by attractive old brick and dense plantings of shrubs to create a very pleasant setting near the house.

THE PLAN

This pool was contoured into the site using a curving, natural lagoon-style shape, and the surrounding area edged and paved in brick to suit the style of the house. Because the garden is level, height both for privacy and protection from prevailing winds has been provided by fast-growing evergreens and by raising the pool wall along one side. This has permitted the installation of a well-planted raised bed and a very effective waterfall feature. A selection of evergreen ferns and reeds complete the planting plan without the risk of leaf-fall polluting the water. A large heated spa has been cleverly integrated into the curve of the pool design, close to the house for ease of use, and it is surrounded by paved patio areas for eating and entertaining on.

1 *Syzygium floribundum*
2 *Camellia japonica*
3 *Nephrolepsis cordifolia*
4 *Eucalyptus citriodora*
5 *Olearia argyrophylla*
6 *Cyathea australis*
7 *Blechnum nudum*
8 *Cyperus papyrus*
9 *Callistemon citrinus*
10 *Melaleuca squamea*
11 *Baeckea linifolia*
12 *Cyperus alternifolius*
13 *Scirpus nodosus*
14 *Tristania conferta*
15 *Asparagus albus*

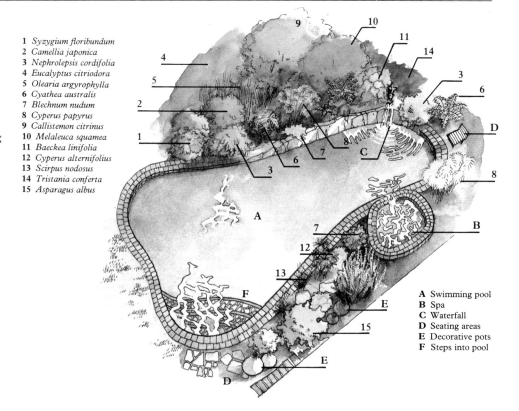

A Swimming pool
B Spa
C Waterfall
D Seating areas
E Decorative pots
F Steps into pool

bathroom and shower facilities beyond in useful proximity to the spa and swimming pool areas.

On the far side of the garden, the pool wall has been raised and backfilled to add height and create a fine backdrop to the pool, and provide complete privacy from surrounding houses. Lavishly planted with free-flowering shrubs, such as azaleas, and with some larger trees and shrubs behind, it provides massed green foliage or a riot of color, depending on the season. To add to the naturalized effect and to focus attention on the dense planting behind the pool, a small waterfall cascades out of the undergrowth and into the deep end. As well as 'softening' this corner of the pool, it strengthens the naturalized appearance of the feature and also adds movement and visual interest to the garden as a whole. The sound of running water is an additional bonus, and the waterfall is very popular with the children and their friends.

Planting round the pool is designed to encourage a lush, watery feel and produce reflections in the water to make up for the fact that plants cannot be positioned at the water's edge. Huge evergreen lillypillies make a dramatic, dense green frame for the planting design; these native Australian trees are prolific growers and produce pink-purple berries up to 13mm/½in in diameter, which are extremely popular with birds. They are heat tolerant with a slightly weeping habit, making them attractive near water both for their fine appearance and the year-round shelter they provide. Closer to the pool is a carefully selected display of different ferns and other moisture-loving plants, each one chosen to exhibit a variety of magnificent types of foliage and shades of green as a foil to the brilliant blue of the water itself. The soil level of the raised, backfilled bed is set slightly below the level of the retaining wall so that soil cannot be washed down.

In order to keep the water free from leaves during autumn, evergreen types only have been included near the pool. These include the spiky reed papyrus and the feathery fishbone fern. More ferns, reeds and grasses have been planted in pots and scattered round the paved area, creating sheltered segregated sunbathing and entertaining areas. These, combined with the owners' beautiful collection of terracotta and earthenware pots and urns, fully complement the rich, earthy tones of the antique brick surround, producing an unexpectedly pleasant and peaceful setting in an urban environment.

BELOW *The pool wall has been raised along one side and backfilled to provide attractive yet very practicable planting beds around the main pool.*

RIGHT *A heated spa pool, raised slightly above the level of the main pool, tucks into the overall design. It is screened by evergreen plants and terracotta planters.*

SPECIAL FEATURES

*How to add practical and attractive finishing touches to a
water feature including design ideas for streams and
watercourses, waterfalls and cascades, fountains and water
sculptures; stepping stones and bridges; paving and other
surface materials; special lighting effects*

ANYONE WHO has taken the time and trouble to design and construct a water garden will be tempted to add special features such as a fountain or waterfall, a stream crossed perhaps by a bridge, a waterside deck or sitting area, or underwater lighting. Lack of space need not be a restriction: a trickle of water sparkling over a brick wall or an arrangement of pebbles into a small patio pool can offer the same satisfaction as a full-scale stream or waterfall in a large, naturalistic garden; the feature can be the focal point of a small design or subtly integrated into a larger one. The important thing is that any feature you choose remains in keeping with the size and style of your pond, garden and the surrounding landscape, and is constructed from sympathetic materials. An ornate fountain oversplashing a too small formal pool, or a small stream lost in the undergrowth of a large, informal water garden will do nothing to enhance their settings.

It helps if you can make an imaginative sketch of the feature in its proposed setting; alternatively, if art isn't your strong point, superimpose an impression of the feature, drawn on a tracing paper overlay, onto a photograph of the intended site. You will find that simple ideas work best in both formal and informal settings: fussy or elaborate designs may spoil the line and design of the whole plan. Before you opt for a particular feature, assess whether it could be successfully adapted to your own garden and be scrupulously accurate in your measurements – mistakes with costly materials will mount up. Enthusiasm and originality are important but must be tempered by common sense. All too often a perfectly good feature is ruined by being in the wrong setting, simply because the owner took a fancy to it: there is no point in installing an oriental bamboo bridge in a classic English country-style garden unless you have other oriental features to which it can relate, for example a pagoda, ginger jars or tubs of bamboo. The Japanese garden on p. 27 works well in a suburban setting because the oriental theme is carried through both house and garden.

Don't be afraid to draw on various sources for inspiration and ideas: pictures in books and magazines are fine, but it sometimes helps to see such features in situ to study their performance, the atmosphere they create and also the sound they make. Visit gardens open to the public and get advice from people who have built something similar, or chat to builders with relevant experience. If you can afford it, you can contact a landscape designer who will give you the ideas and even carry out the whole design for you. Fountains, waterfalls, bridges and lighting are, after all, functional as well as ornamental and so need careful planning and installation if they are to fulfill both their practical and aesthetic roles.

Your terrain, the availability of materials and your budget will largely dictate the style of your special feature. Make good use of natural contours like hillocks, dips and mounds; a bank of earth makes the perfect setting for a waterfall, with the addition of boulders and bold planting.

Some of the best, most satisfying ideas are created using the simplest, cheapest components. Look around for second-hand or leftover materials from other projects: old railroad ties, drainage pipes, tiles, bricks and stones, and consider how they might be used imaginatively in your water garden. If the material is sturdy enough and creates the right ambiance, by all means adapt it to your needs. You may find that local materials cost less and they will almost certainly look more in keeping than 'foreign' ones.

Another way to make a water garden harmonize with the general design is to take account of the materials already used in surrounding buildings or surfaces. A brick-built bridge or watercourse matching the house walls, a paved formal pool as part of the patio, or a wooden deck continuing the theme of timbering in a Tudor or timber-framed clapboard house, are examples of how such features might be integrated.

ABOVE *However small, a formal pool can add interest to a corner of the garden. Here, a well-weathered mill wheel is the centerpiece and planting is restricted to beds and pots in and around the paving.*

RIGHT *A variety of leaf shapes and soft-colored flowers create a lovely wild effect, giving the impression of a meandering stream crossed by a simple, low wooden bridge.*

MOVING WATER

One of the great pleasures of creating a water garden is the opportunity to feature moving water. Waterfalls, fountains and streams may cost more and take more effort to install and maintain than a pond or still water canal, but the pleasure you will get from them makes them thoroughly rewarding. Nothing can really compare with the visual excitement of cascading or splashing water and the way it catches and changes the light, or the relaxing qualities of the constant sound – an excellent way to mask irritating urban noises. In addition, moving water means more oxygen, which is helpful in promoting wildlife, as the water is then also less likely to freeze over in winter. Debris is carried away by the flow, so cleaning is made easier.

Your moving water feature needn't be large or elaborate, but you will need a steady source of water, either fed naturally by a stream or spring or artificially recycled by a pump (see pp. 132-4). You may also need some means of topping up the water level in hot weather, and somewhere for excess water to drain away if the level rises too high during wet weather (see p. 129).

Planning and installation need equal care if the feature is to work successfully (see pp. 124-31). In particular, when you are designing a flow of water from one area to another, practicalities are important. Too fast a flow and the water rushes away; too slow and you may get blockages and overflows. Streams must be lined to prevent water leaking and be wide enough not to inhibit the flow. Yet, if a stream is too wide and too steep, the water will flow too fast and overspill the sides. Waterfalls must not drop from too great a height or you will not be able to replace quickly enough the volume of water lost. When assessing the size of the feature, remember that the bigger it is the greater the volume of water.

If you are lucky enough to have a natural source of running water in your garden – a stream, a spring or seepage from a rock face – you will have to monitor it over a period of at least one year to check that it has neither too little water during dry periods nor too much during wet ones. Check that the supply is not polluted by tracing it back toward the source if possible, noting any farms or overflows from drains and sewers, septic tanks or chlorinated swimming pools, all of which may wreak havoc on plants and fish. Unfortunately, natural water supplies are never predictable so even if you can pronounce yours clear, be prepared for heavy rains or floods upstream that can wash polluted material out of ditches or bring sewage downstream.

This blend of formal and informal design relies on natural materials and dense planting. A circular paved island echoes the curve of the water.

– Streams and Watercourses –

A stream or watercourse in the garden neither requires a very large area nor need it be particularly deep; a narrow watercourse, with a flow about 4cm/1.5in deep, can be used to divide off a particular part of the garden, or a small stream gurgling over a visible bed of pebbles can be just as effective as larger, more ambitious versions of them. But, with larger streams, there is the added pleasure of seeing water flow under bridges or around stepping stones, and this, too, you can emulate in your own garden (see pp. 64-9).

Creating a natural-looking stream with grassy banks, or with rocky banks using pebbles and boulders, is very much a matter of trial and error. It helps if you can study a stream in its natural state to get an idea of shape, size and flow. Water will always take the line of least resistance, going round solid obstacles and through softer rocks such as limestone, with falls and weirs changing the pace of its flow. The bends and breaks caused by solid objects are the features that you will be trying to imitate to make your stream look as natural as possible; note exactly how the boulders are positioned and how the water reacts to them, the shape and sequence of the curves. The Japanese, in creating their gardens, have always been acutely aware of natural forms in rocky landscapes, and it is worth studying photographs of their 'stream' gardens. Invariably, they will show dry streams – winding courses of pebbles or rocks which concentrate on the form and shape of a stream rather than the water itself.

Gentle curves and grassy banks help naturalize this shallow stream. Low-growing evergreen shrubs and mossy rocks and boulders add plenty of visual interest.

Streams need a good, steady supply of water to flow well, and for this you will need a pump capable of circulating the volume of water to the top of the course (see pp. 132-4). To prevent the water rushing too fast, the stream bed should be flat, for the pump will perform the function of a natural stream's flow. You can, of course, add interest with little pools and weirs along the stream's course that allow the water to build up and spill over (see Waterfalls and cascades, below). You can increase the speed of the flow by narrowing the channel with larger rocks.

Landscaping your stream in the context of the rest of your garden needs careful planning, too. Using it to link either two ponds or two waterfalls, or a pond and a waterfall, or a formal and an informal water feature, always works well. If you want to use the stream itself as a focal point, try to position it so that it runs away from the chief viewpoint, not across it; that way the eye can gaze along a whole length of water, and not just glance across its width – far more dramatic. Softening the edges with suitable waterside plants (see pp. 100-11) and crossing it with one or two bridges or stepping stones can help enhance the natural effect.

Whereas the stream should aim to look as natural as possible, the watercourse is a formal, artificial device, evolving partly from the moated castle and manor house, but also from much more ancient artefacts. If you look closely at oriental carpet designs you will often see a recurring theme of a garden divided into four parts by means of straight water channels. The watercourse is very common in the water gardens dating from the Mogul period in India, and it is an excellent device for breaking a garden plot up into more interesting shapes. Don't think only of dividing the garden widthwise – use the watercourse to divide it lengthwise and even diagonally.

To line a watercourse, you can use compressed clay, concrete or a butyl liner. The straight sides can be of concrete, brick, turf or seasoned lumber. Turf is more time-consuming to maintain, but creates a more natural look for an informal garden. The flow of water can be very shallow, but the sides should be high enough to prevent water spilling over. Mogul watercourses very often have patterned bottoms over which the water flows steadily at a depth of no more than a centimeter or two, and you don't have to be an expert stonemason to include a simple watercourse studded with decorative mosaic tiles or simple designs of small cemented pebbles.

DESIGNING A WATERCOURSE

The channels of a watercourse should be slightly larger than necessary for the volume of water that is to flow in them, to allow for rainwater. In addition, provision should be made for a simple overflow system to a part of the garden that can accommodate any surplus water. Here, overhanging paving slabs break up the straight channels without restricting the flow.

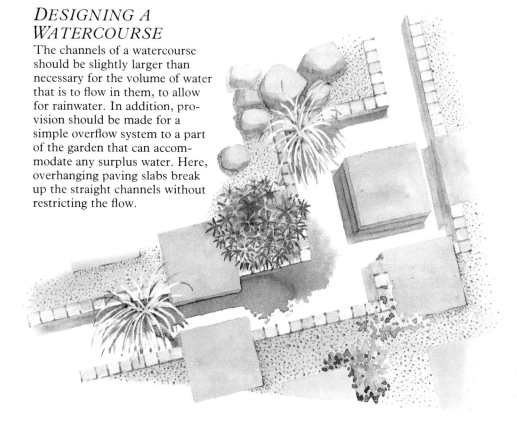

– WATERFALLS AND CASCADES –

There is something exciting about waterfalls and cascades – perhaps it's to do with the exhilarating sight of water bubbling over or bouncing off rocks, the air hung with a fine spray, and the accompanying sound of the water's roar, or just its tinkling trickle. In a garden it is usually better not to have too high a waterfall as it is difficult (and expensive) to make it

A natural waterfall looks at its best spilling over a shallow stepped arrangement of boulders. Here, tall trees and an elegant shelter provide necessary height and form.

look natural, and you will need to circulate a very great volume of water. A modest, natural-looking waterfall as part of a rockery, or a concrete cascade built into a patio pool, or even a simple trickle of water issuing from a slot or fissure to run down the natural slope of a wall, will give just as much pleasure and fewer installation problems.

Any mountainous or hilly area should give you ideas for a waterfall. There are as many types of waterfall as there are ways of arranging rocks, and the illustrations below show a few of them only. The height of the fall and the type of rocks you use below your waterfall will affect its sound; if it is very high it may be too noisy, create too much splashing and lose water too quickly. A top-up tank may be needed to keep the water supply constant. As with building the stream, the only way to build a successful waterfall is to experiment, adjusting the position of a boulder or rock here or there until you are happy with the effect. It is therefore wise not to mortar stones in position too soon, since you could make extra work for yourself.

Small waterfalls often fit rather well into rockeries, and are indeed very popular in smaller gardens. Yet they invariably disappoint their owners because of the huge amount of water they lose. The secret is to ensure that the stones are lined behind with butyl liner so that water cannot seep down the back. Preformed fiberglass saucers can be bought which, sunk between the boulders, can be used for a series of cascades. The rocks would still need lining first, however. It is important to ensure that the saucers are not too shallow, or the water splashes over the edges, washing away the soil.

TYPES OF WATERFALL

When deciding on materials for a waterfall, it is most important that your rocks look as natural as possible: local stone will be most in keeping. With an overhanging fall, you should create a lip at the top of the waterfall so that the water does not trickle down the back of the rocks. Apart from rock or stone, consider using tiles, bricks or even clear fiberglass.

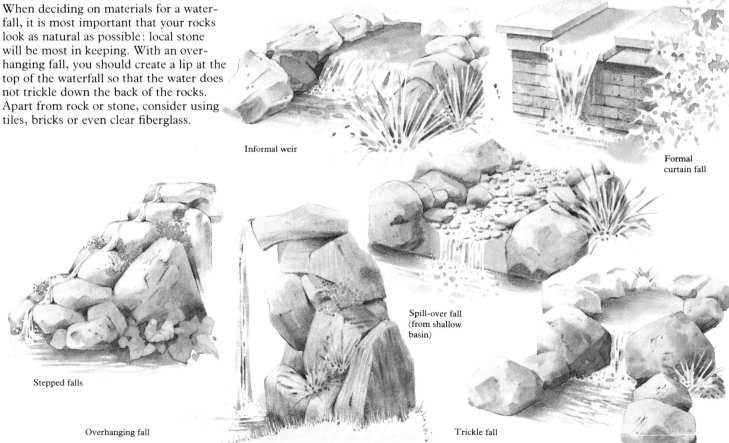

Informal weir

Formal curtain fall

Spill-over fall (from shallow basin)

Stepped falls

Overhanging fall

Trickle fall

Water spouting at intervals from regular gaps between these tiled steps falls in an attractive cascade into a formal pool, with raised beds softening hard edges and providing plant interest.

Using soil from a pool excavation is a good and economical way to create some of the height required for a waterfall feature; the effect of height can be emphasized by large boulders and dense background plants such as bamboo, *Fatsia japonica* and *Mahonia japonica*.

In a formal setting, perhaps a patio water garden, the wild, haphazard effect of the naturalistic rocky waterfall tends to look rather out of place. Sloping open channels or watercourses, with the water fast-flowing yet controlled, are more in keeping. A Mogul idea from India, and one popular in medieval formal gardens, is a small cascade issuing from regularly placed openings in a brick or stone wall. This can look very pretty in a paved or walled pool garden, and can be as simple or elaborate as you wish.

In larger formal gardens, perhaps close by the house where concrete, brick and stone features go well, regular contained pools at different levels look stunning linked by a series of cascades, edged with concrete, brick or seasoned lumber. Alternatively, a length of half channel piping (the kind used to protect service pipes underground) can spill out abruptly into a simple pool. Or, if you have already constructed streams or watercourses in your garden, you can amuse yourself for hours with that popular pastime of children – constructing weirs and dams to create a terraced effect of small falls. Experiment with different lengths and heights of wooden planks to restrict or increase the flow of water.

Be adventurous with your choice of materials but remember that they must be well treated to withstand the constant flow of water (see pp. 148-51).

– FOUNTAINS AND WATER SCULPTURES –
Fountains have always been one of the most popular ornamental water features, producing plumes or sprays of water to catch and diffuse the light before tumbling back into a pool. They are useful for adding height and interest to the water garden and come in a huge range of types and styles from abstract designs to bowls, boxes, animals, birds, fish and so on. Try not to be seduced by something that will look totally out of place in your garden: many fountains are gimmicky and badly made, others simply copies of famous fountains like the ubiquitous Brussels Boy. Avoid all the plastic, cheaply-made monstrosities – they do little to enhance the garden, show no creativity on your

part and have nothing in common with the natural landscape.

The best fountain effects can be achieved with the three-tier bowl type, made of ceramic or concrete. This creates a classical effect but is not too elaborate for a small garden; even an average-sized backyard can display a simple fountain feature such as a trickling water spout. Anyone who has been to Rome will have been amazed by the beautiful fountains squeezed into unlikely street corners. On a more modest scale, an old water pump, an old-fashioned tap or even a hole in a brick wall, with one brick overhanging the

others, produce interesting variations on the theme. Alternatively, why not tuck a simple bubble fountain into the corner of the patio? This type has a small pump concealed within a shallow well underground and produces a steady bubble of water over pebbles or cobbles (see pp. 132-4). This type of fountain is particularly suitable if you have young children as the water reservoir is stored underground rather than above it, yet you still have the advantage of the sight and sound of moving water.

Although the standard of some of the more elaborate fountains has declined with mass production, there has been an

exciting show of interest in moving water by sculptors the world over, many of whom have been inspired to produce works that have water playing around and over them: a bronze girl with an umbrella stands beneath a perpetual shower; sci-fi globes bob on the water's surface; fine jets of water cross and re-cross to create fascinating geometric patterns. Bronze, stone, glass (but avoid colored glass), clear fiberglass and chrome – the possibilities are limited only by the artist's imagination.

It can be difficult to find exactly the right spot for a piece of sculpture, and it is worth bearing in mind that there are

This unusual water sculpture is operated by a simple concealed hose spout, with the water circulated by means of a pump situated in the tub. Ferns and leafy plants, such as Fatsia japonica, *grown in pots, provide a gentle, leafy setting for the sculpture.*

Bubble fountain
A bubble fountain is perfect for any situation where you don't want an exposed stretch of water, since the sump is concealed underground. Here, water bubbles over an old millstone surrounded by pebbles that hide the grating over the sump.

no rules – you will know instinctively when it looks right. However, in an urban or formal garden it often helps to position it in front of a trellis or wall, both to frame it and set it off. Long grass and low, trailing plants can be trained to hide the base, while trees and shrubs make a useful backdrop. Some sculptures look better surrounded by rocks and shingle to emphasize their dramatic qualities. Large, architectural plants can also look very good alongside bold sculptures. It helps to live with your sculpture for a while and get used to the mood it generates before deciding on its best setting. Don't be afraid to set it near the house – it can often provide the perfect link between house and garden.

ABOVE '*Ripple Wall*' *by sculptor William Pye makes full use of the reflective quality of water through its clever combination of vertical lines and curves. The rectangular lines of the brick columns appear to go right to the bottom of the pool, while the lines of the semicircles are made whole by their reflection.*

LEFT *The soft, silver finish to this modern fountain sculpture makes it equally suited to both formal and informal pools. The principle is simple and the effect very pleasing : a pyramid, punctured with holes and fed from the base, provides a fine grid of moving water.*

CROSSING WATER

A bridge or stepping stones across a stream are natural additions, and well designed and carefully placed they also add interest to any larger stretch of water. A small jetty or wooden deck (see p. 70) can be equally effective. Apart from being attractive features in themselves, they can add another dimension, offering the chance to view the garden from new angles: the opposite bank, an island, or simply the middle of the water. For this reason, stepping stones and bridges should be wide enough for you to stand on comfortably. Stepping stones should be spaced to encourage a leisurely crossing and must be safe for old people and children to use. They should be just wide enough to allow only one person to cross

STEPPING STONES

Stepping stones should never run in a straight line but should be laid so that they form a pattern. Try to place the long axis of each step at right angles to the direction of the path you are making. Follow concave shapes with convex ones, and angle flat edges against one another, to give the stones a continuous motion. Slabs of 'crazy paving,' concrete paving slabs, sections of wooden deck and sawn and treated sections of log all make attractive-looking steps.

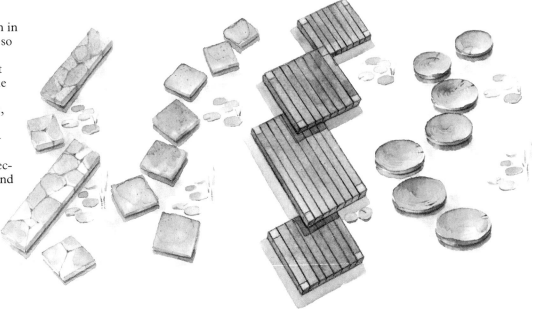

at a time, and positioned according to an average or even small natural step – it is better to have too many rather than too few. Larger bridges should be strong enough to support three or four people at one time and at least 60cm/24in wide.

The most sensible place to position a bridge or stepping stones is where the contour of a pool or stream suggests a natural crossing point. But try, if you can, to alter slightly the direction of stepping stones or angle a bridge rather than run them in a rigidly straight line across the water – it will be pleasanter on the eye.

– STEPPING STONES –

Stepping stones originally evolved as a simple means of crossing water without building a bridge, as anyone who has attempted to cross a remote mountain stream will appreciate. In Japan they became an important feature of 'dry' gardens adjoining the ritual tea-rooms, where the formal yet natural arrangement of the stones was seen to be aesthetically pleasing. In the water garden, too, stepping stones can encourage appreciation of the environment by forcing a slower walking pace and, as the eyes are turned downward to ensure a safe footing, by allowing the passerby to stop and look into the water. They are mainly laid across streams rather than deeper ponds and pools, and, if a natural, moving water feature such as a cascade or small waterfall has been incorporated, the movement of water around the stones can be most attractive.

Choice of materials for stepping stones is important, as each step should be even and not too slippery. Choose from formal-cut paving slabs, irregular flat-topped stones or even log slices and wooden boards. Arrange them carefully to achieve a pleasing design. Mixing and matching stones and materials can be rewarding but it generally takes some trial and error before the sequence looks right. You may find it easier to work out the design to scale on graph paper first, rather than lift heavy stones or slabs in and out of the water. Even better, especially when trying to visualize the design from every angle, cut out the shapes in card or paper and play around with them on your lawn or even your living-room carpet. It is also worth remembering that the farther apart the steps are laid, the quicker one tends to walk across them. With careful thought, you can use a large stone or several placed together to create places to pause where there is a feature or view of particular interest.

Stones and concrete slabs can, if necessary, be anchored in concrete to keep them stable, and at all times they should be kept free from moss, algae and other slippery substances. Wooden steps or blocks may need regular scouring with a stiff wire brush to keep their surface clean and slip-free. Strategically placed surface-water plants, such as lilies and mosses, will help soften the lines of any stepping stones, provided they are not allowed to encroach too far over the slabs.

RIGHT *Based on simple lines, this bridge fits in well with its natural setting. Treated wooden steps and planking are embellished by an attractive handrail with diagonal supports.*

– BRIDGES –

Basic, unfussy bridge designs usually look best and are stronger and more stable than complex ones. The latter often indicate poor structure or workmanship. A simple, well-balanced bridge – it need only be a few planks, or a log secured on either bank, or low wooden scaffolding just above the waterlevel – is attractive, cheaper, and easier to build than an elaborate, ornamental structure. Keeping it low also encourages eye contact with the water for observing fish and plants. Higher, arched bridges are really only required when boats pass underneath and, unless you need one for that purpose, you are advised to leave well alone. They are fairly complicated to construct and need the assistance and advice of a skilled workman.

A tip worth remembering, if you are having a wooden bridge specially made, is to have it built slightly longer than required; the visual effect will be to widen the stream. Also, if the banks should erode, you will be able to move the bridge to a slightly wider part of the water.

There are some ideas for good, simple bridge designs on p. 68. These can be adapted to most settings and show how very basic stone and wood materials can be used effectively.

Provided your chosen surface is kept nonslip, a handrail or sides are not absolutely necessary, but you may prefer to add this safety feature if young children or the elderly will be using the bridge. It is also useful to have something

RIGHT *This style of bridge encourages a leisurely crossing and allows plenty of space to pause and contemplate the garden.*

to lean against if your bridge is positioned at a good viewing place.

While style and safety will be your primary considerations when designing bridges, choice of materials will be dictated by your budget. Unfortunately, the best so far as performance and looks are concerned are stone and hardwoods, which are also the most expensive. You will probably have to compromise with cheaper softwoods and other materials. However, there is no need to compromise on good design and you can still achieve a harmonious effect, provided you don't use too many different, contrasting types and textures of material. A plank top on a brick base, or mismatching lumber disguised by being stained a soft blue or dark brown, are perfectly acceptable.

Wood probably makes the simplest and most effective type of bridge: it is easy to work with, relatively inexpensive and wonderfully versatile. Your bridge can be as simple as a single plank supported by a length of tree-trunk sunk into the stream bed in the center, or old, sound, inexpensive railroad ties held together with planks secured underneath, and with each end buried in soil or concrete.

For a more complex bridge, wooden deck walks can look very stunning, used to link wider platform areas separated by stretches of water, with the wood laid in different directions to create interesting patterns.

Stone bridges, suspended by means of a central pier or keystone, or several of them, are generally expensive and take time to build. They must be carefully designed and expertly built to look good and stand firm. However, a single granite slab, if you are lucky enough to acquire one, slung low across a small stream and wedged into the bank on both sides, makes a splendid, simple bridge. Large, old millstones also make an excellent natural-looking bridge, safely supported and just skimming the water level.

Unless you are already experienced with the medium, concrete is best avoided in bridge building. It normally requires forming with lumber to support the wet concrete as it is poured, and reinforcing with steel bars.

A brick bridge is far simpler to build and looks particularly good if your water feature is close to a building of harmonizing brick. If the bridge is away from the house or other brickwork, choose paler buffs and yellows, blues or grays rather than reds and russets, as the former tend to look better against the water.

The most effective style of brick bridge is a system of one or two shallow arches supported on concrete piers as close to the water as possible, with grass and plants grown to cover the concrete footings. If, however, you are a novice bricklayer, do not attempt this yourself.

TYPES OF BRIDGE

Even quite wide stretches of water can be crossed using very simply designed bridges. Wooden planks used widthwise tend to make the bridge look shorter, while planks used lengthwise make it appear longer (as well as using less wood). Large pieces of flat stone can also be used to cross shallow water, as long as the bed is extremely even.

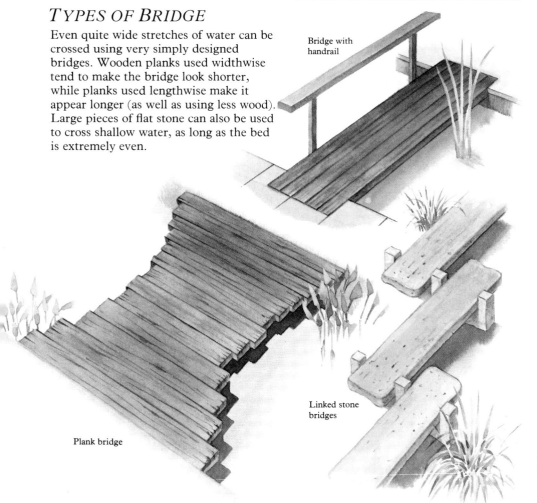

Bridge with handrail

Plank bridge

Linked stone bridges

ABOVE *A simple wood-planked bridge is perfect for an informal water garden. The bridge is set slightly off-center to lessen the symmetry between it and the pond.*

RIGHT *A wide wood-planked walk, resting just above the water's surface, stretches across a large natural pond. Its proximity to the water makes it easier to examine the plants more closely and creates an unobtrusive natural feature.*

PAVING & SURROUNDS

◆

A pool's immediate surroundings can add impact and emphasis rather than blend into the background – a useful device for small ponds but one that needs to be handled skillfully. Rough grass, wild flowers and large waterside plants (see pp. 100-11) may be the perfect setting for a large naturalistic pond, but to surround a formal, geometric pool with them will seem like neglect. A wide wooden or stone coping or a slightly raised brick edge around a small, formal pool will make it look larger and more important, as will irregular stone slabs or boulders round a small, informal pond.

There is such a range of suitable materials for pond surrounds that it can be difficult to visualize what might suit your garden best. Narrow the choice by taking your lead from the general style and atmosphere of your house and garden; the surround must not only create a practical and attractive edge to the water, but also form a visual link with other features.

Seasoned wood can be adapted to suit many styles, formal and informal; it looks equally good combined with brick or stone near the house or laid in geometric patterns round a formal pool.

When planning any type of surrounding surface, always design it to scale on

Wooden decking is an excellent linking material between house and pool. Here, the deck has been built out over the water to create a quayside effect.

graph paper first. This way you can check that it looks right, making sure that you minimize the number of cut slabs or tiles, and that you can afford to buy the materials. If you find the cost beyond your budget, consider using the more expensive materials in smaller quantities, combined with a cheaper but compatible surface. Try not to use more than two contrasting materials – such as wooden decking across paving, or wood and stone stepping stones across grass – or closely related materials, such as slabs, stones and cobbles.

– WOODEN DECKING –

As has already been said, wooden decking is an excellent sympathetic material for surrounding both formal and informal pools. It is softer and more mellow than paving, more practical and cleaner underfoot than grass or shingle, and combines well with wooden rails, seats, pergolas and other structures. Hardwoods such as redwood and red cedar are the best type of lumber for outdoors, being highly resistant to splintering, warping and decay. However, unless you have a local supply, they tend to be very expensive

In a more formal setting, decks can look superb laid in overlapping levels with the planks set at different angles to form interesting patterns.

and you are more likely to use a softwood, for example pine, larch or spruce, all of which will need treatment with a suitable preservative. It is important that the surface remains nonslip in wet weather and it may need roughening with a wire brush from time to time.

A deck can be arranged in simple or elaborate designs according to the style of your garden. It can be laid diagonally, in blocks or even in complicated herringbone patterns. Use it to build out from the house to link living areas with the pool, or to create interesting changes of level between pools, using a stepped scaffolding effect.

A handrail or balustrade can be both an attractive safety feature and a place to lean and gaze out over the water from. Tubs of plants and pots on the deck and spaces left for planting at the water's margins as well as on dry land will all help soften the straight lines of the wood. The Japanese-style garden on p. 28 and the garden on p. 45 show how effectively wooden decks can be used as a framework for water, plants and other features in very different settings.

Softening edges
Sections of wooden deck look particularly good if a small gap is left for pebbles and plants.

– GRASS –

Grass is an obvious choice for large, landscaped informal ponds and lakes. It loves moisture and will flourish right up to the water's edge, indeed anywhere that provides sufficient light (too much shade under trees will leave you with bare patches). Despite this fondness for water, grassed areas should be drained towards the pond or pool to prevent them becoming too boggy – a gradient of 1:80 should be sufficient. You can allow the grass to grow long, attractively seeded with wild flowers, or, for a more orderly and formal effect, you can clip and mow the grass to a fine finish.

– ROCK AND GRAVEL –

For a wilder, craggy effect to set off informal pools, rough stones and large boulders, perhaps combined with an alpine garden and waterfall, can look very impressive even on a modest scale. This type of landscape only really looks good in an informal garden and you will have to be prepared to spend some time experimenting with the separate components until it looks right. Trial and error with scaled-down models or even pebbles saves heaving heavy boulders around. Using local stone will help this kind of garden landscape look more natural. The stone should always be laid

according to its natural strata and softened with carefully placed plants to integrate it with the rest of the garden.

For areas of heavy shade around informal pools, shattered rock, pebbles or gravel create an excellent natural background. As to stone color, there is a wide range to choose from depending on the effect you hope to achieve, from moody blues and grays to soft whites and browns. Add one or two large boulders and plants like *Lysimachia* or *Alchemilla mollis* that will grow easily in gravel, for contrast and change of texture. Or, you could create a shingle beach that slopes gently into the water.

The drawback of pebble and gravel pond-side areas is that they require rather

A gently sloping shingle or gravel beach is extremely popular for Japanese-style water features, and makes a fine neutral background for more dramatic features.

SURFACE MATERIALS

Choice of materials to use with your water feature will largely depend on the style of the rest of your garden. If mixing different types of material, keep them simple and restrict your choice to only two or, sometimes, three examples.

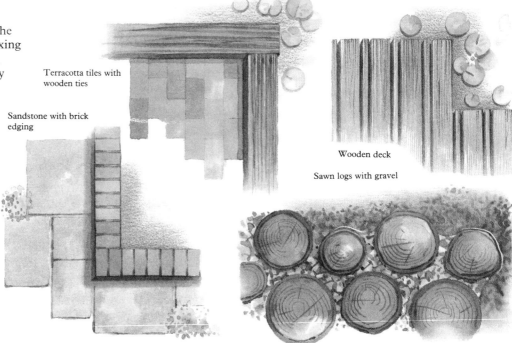

Terracotta tiles with wooden ties

Wooden deck

Sawn logs with gravel

Belgian blocks with raised pool surround

Sandstone with brick edging

more effort to maintain than many other surfaces. Unless they form a beach, you will need to contain them with some kind of edging (wood or concrete) to prevent the stones falling into the pond. They will need regular leveling and weeding as rainwater and wear and tear take their toll, and occasional topping up. But in the right setting the effort is well worthwhile for the fine natural effect created.

– Bark –

Cheaper than gravel and best suited to woodland areas are bark chips, which will not support annual weeds and which look very good under trees as well as being practical underfoot. They cannot be laid right up to the water's edge as they will be washed away, but with a wood edging, and round blocks of wood set into the chips like stepping stones, to break up large areas, they make an inexpensive but natural surface. The chips will need topping up about every six months if they get a lot of wear. In autumn sweep them regularly with a soft twiggy broom to clear off leaves before they become sodden.

– Paving and Bricks –

An obvious choice of surround for more formal and patio pools is paving. It is not cheap or easy to install, but it is quick and simple to maintain and should last for years providing it is frost-resistant. The choice of surface is wide and varied and you should consider both color and texture very carefully before buying, to ensure that it harmonizes with both

Large, rough stones are useful for disguising the edges of small informal pools and can be interplanted with grass and creeping plants.

house and garden. Simple patterns and natural colors work best and will not detract either from the water feature or from any tubs and pots you wish to stand on the surface. Avoid whitened finishes – when sited next to water they give off glare in strong sunshine. Paving can be rough- or smooth-textured and, as a general rule, the finer the finish the more formal the effect.

Slabs are widely available in regular squares, sometimes 'pointed' into brick or tile effects, but they can be circular or hexagonal-shaped. The cheapest type of paving is concrete-based, but look out for stone slabs which give a far more natural effect; they are expensive, and if you are trying to economize, use them over a smaller area combined with grass or lumber. Tennessee fieldstone paving slabs are beautiful and readily available as well as being comparatively straightforward to lay. Large slabs can be interplanted with herbs and grasses.

Belgian blocks are extremely hard-wearing and create a good, unobtrusive finish that gives off a wonderful steely-gray shine when wet. For a warmer, more mellow effect, sandstone is available in many textures from smooth-surfaced sawn slabs to craggy 'random' and 'dressed' pieces. Rough stones or cobbles (round, egg-shaped stones) can be set in mortar for a rather rough, uneven finish, useful for creating a change of texture among smooth pavings, but they are not really practical to stand furniture on.

Hard-wearing bricks are an excellent foil for most ponds and pools – use the yellower tones or old, already weathered brick for a more mellow effect and the reds to match an existing wall surface. You can create all kinds of patterns with bricks, such as herringbone or basket-weave edged with upended bricks (called a soldier course). Don't create too elaborate a design or it may distract attention from the water feature.

MATCHING POOL AND SURROUND

Your pool surround is as important a design consideration as the water feature itself. For a formal brick-edged pool, for example, a brick surface can provide the perfect surround. For a less-formal feature, you can use a mixture of materials, while a wooden deck is useful for providing a change of height.

Formal brick pool

Informal pool

Split-level deck and brick

1 'Crazy paving'
2 Ties overhanging water
3 Pebble beach
4 Large rocks
5 Pebbles set in concrete
6 Paving slabs

LEFT *A combination of materials will work if they are used sympathetically. Here, the wooden deck laid across the brick surround overlaps the pool and creates a new level. The wood follows the direction of the brick and compliments its mellow warmth.*

RIGHT *Large frost-proof quarry tiles add warmth and a change of texture to this formal water garden. The color and smoothness of the tiles are perfect for a small, square eating and seating area beside the lush pool plants and the surrounding greenery.*

LIGHTING

◆

All types of garden benefit from being lit at night and a good, carefully installed system of lighting will not only extend the use of the garden in summer for parties, barbecues, swimming and alfresco meals, but can provide an illuminated showpiece of shadow and silhouette visible from the house in colder months. With a water feature, the disadvantage of having to avoid glare from lights beamed directly on to the water is outweighed by the wonderful opportunities to illuminate dramatic waterside plants like *Gunnera* and *Petasites*, or to reflect a tree or building in a calm, dark stretch of water.

The restrictions on fitting effective garden lighting are financial. It has to be installed safely (see pp. 142-3), and this is always labor-intensive and requires expert help and advice; the fittings are expensive owing to their safety and durability requirements. In some countries they can be difficult and costly to get hold of, too, except through specialist lighting companies. Lights near or attached to the house are naturally less expensive, reducing the amount of cable used. You can buy DIY lighting kits which include everything you need but they usually restrict you to one lighting effect. A wide range of cheap waxed flares and candles is readily available, some of which discourage insects, and Chinese lanterns and bamboo flares with refillable oil

A combination of lighting effects highlighting different features in the water garden has successfully illuminated the whole area simultaneously.

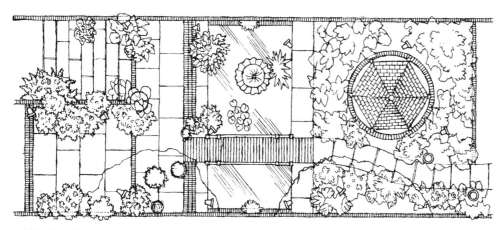

Lighting plan
The plan of the lighting scheme for the garden shown opposite can be seen here. The combined use of uplighters, floodlights and spotlights can, if required, completely illuminate the garden at night. Used selectively, however, these lights can create a more intimate atmosphere.

Floodlights and spotlights   Lights with integral ground spikes   Uplighters

LIGHTING EFFECTS

To get a good idea of what different lighting effects look like in the garden before you carry out any expensive installation, take a spotlight on a length of cable and try it out in various positions. The lit features will have to look good from different viewpoints – not just from the house – and fitments should be concealed wherever possible by burying them in the ground or positioning them behind rocks and plants. All-round lighting is usually more successful than directional lighting, which highlights a feature from only one angle, and avoid shining light directly onto the water since this tends to emphasize any dirt or muddiness.

1

2

3

4

1 Lighting under decks or bridges
2 Spotlighting special features
3 Overhead pool lighting
4 Bridge lighting

reservoirs are a useful novelty for oriental-style gardens. But none of these is a substitute for a properly planned and safely installed electric outdoor lighting system. It is important that fitments should not be seen during daylight, unless they are attractive enough, like some path lights and wall lamps, to create a garden feature, and you should make sure they can be carefully concealed behind rocks, shrubs and plants without obscuring the beam of light.

Most lighting systems are variations

of a few basic weatherproof fitments: concealed underground well-lights (neat and unobtrusive but sometimes rather difficult to get hold of); sturdy spotlights which can be fixed to the ground, preferably hidden by a plant or a slightly raised mound of soil or lawn, or attached to a tree or building; raised lamps for 'spread lighting' or for creating pools of light over low plants or along patios; and waterproof low-voltage underwater lights for pools, fountains and other water features. All these lights are generally

available in one of three types: popular tungsten which gives a warm, yellow light; more expensive discharge lighting using sodium or mercury for a bluish-green tinted light (very complimentary for lighting plants and water); and low-voltage tungsten halogen lights, which need a transformer but produce a very white light that brings out the natural color of plants. You will be far more successful in controlling your lighting effects with these three different types of lamp equipment than by attempting to use colored bulbs or filters; a multitude of reds, greens and blues will transform what was a very pleasant pool or pond by day into a crude fairy grotto by night. (Many of the cheaper outdoor lights are fitted with colored covers or filters which you can simply slip off.)

The secret of lighting your water garden subtly and successfully is to build up an overall effect by lighting specific areas individually. Spotlight the seating and eating areas, highlight a few trees, a fountain or statue and, to increase the general lightness of the area, install underwater lighting in the pool itself. You will find that a combination of foreground and background lighting gives a more three-dimensional effect, allowing you to build up areas of interest and create different moods as required. Decide from what vantage point you will be viewing the garden. From the dining room, for example, you should illuminate the obvious focal point in the distance, whereas a patio or swimming pool area needs more immediate pools of light. Ideally, these areas should all be controlled individually so that you can select the effects you require according to your needs. It may be expensive, but well worth it for the flexibility it offers and infinitely better than the flood-lit baseball diamond effect so often seen. In fact, if your lighting plan is well thought out in the early stages, it could cost a lot less than a sudden, even if simple, afterthought later on. You may even find that you need separate lighting systems for summer and winter: for example, either

On this poolside wooden deck, a spotlight has been concealed by terracotta pots of leafy plants, which themselves benefit from the uplighting to create an effective night-time feature.

to light a tree in full foliage or to emphasize its stark silhouette when its branches are bare.

When experimenting with the lighting of pool-surround features, remember to check their reflection in the water as well as from all likely viewpoints. Trees and large plants can be spotlighted from a distance providing they are only going to be viewed from one direction, but the effect tends to be rather flat and two-dimensional. Much better is to uplight, using sunken well-lights or concealed accent lights as close to the object as possible to provide all round lighting and better detailing. Small uplighters hidden in the center of bold architectural plants like *Gunnera* and *Rheum* create interesting shapes and shadows which can look dramatic when reflected in a dark pool of water, while small raised lamps above ground-cover plants or low shrubs cast soft pools of light over a wide, low area of the garden.

For a soft 'moonlight' effect, light shone from both above and below foliage creates interesting dappled patterns on the leaves and on the water or ground below. A dramatic silhouette can be created simply by lighting the wall behind a tree or large shrub – which also gives a striking reflection in the pool in winter. Features such as sculptures and statues, as well as 'white' water from streams and fountains, are best spotlighted directly to bring them into sharp

relief. Many fountains are available with built-in lighting situated beneath a multiholed jet – again, avoid colored lights if you want to maintain a natural effect.

Paths leading to pools or water features can be attractively lit using low-voltage spread-lights, usually freestanding and attractive enough to look good in daylight. These create warm pools of light and, combined with brighter, highervoltage lights picking out shrubs, trees and foliage to either side, the effect is of a soft but varied line of light – very useful and attractive when used on a winding path. Bridges and wooden decks, and also stepping stones, if light fittings are suitable for underwater use, will benefit from this treatment, particularly if the lights can be tucked underneath the structure to create interesting reflections in the water, too. If you have built your pool close to the house, consider lighting the building so that it is reflected in the water. Buildings are best lit from below, as close to the wall as you can get.

Underwater lighting is best used in conjunction with one or more of the lighting systems described above; it will diminish the effect of the lit reflections but add considerably to the overall light of the area – important for parties and night-time swimming.

A swimming pool is one of the rare instances where colored lights can be used successfully – usually from the ceiling of a covered pool complex to create interesting patterns on what can be a large expanse of dark, blank water.

After-dark lighting of a house so that it is reflected in the calm surface of a pool is always successful. This is the deck on p. 70 seen from another angle.

WATER FOR LEISURE

Choosing and installing hot tubs and spas, accessories, plants and surrounds; integrating swimming and splash pools, either together or as separate features, into your garden site; choosing pool surrounds; using water indoors to create an exciting and very different focal point for the home

HOT TUBS & SPAS

A hot tub is principally a wooden container of water kept at a constant temperature, with seats inside and the facility to massage the body with stimulating jets of hot water. If thoughtfully sited and surrounded by interesting plants it will create a handsome feature within a paved or timbered patio area.

A cheaper alternative is a fiberglass spa. They are available in a wide range of shapes and sizes and, although better suited for use indoors, spas can be installed outdoors provided they are built into paving or wooden decks.

– CHOOSING A SITE –

When deciding the location of a tub or spa, the prime consideration must be that the site is strong enough to take the combined weight of the structure, water and bathers – which can be as much as 3628kg/8000lb. A reinforced concrete slab 10 to 15cm/4 to 6in thick should be sufficient to withstand the load, but a tub can also be supported on reinforced concrete piers or wooden joists if you are installing it into a wood-framed floor. If in doubt, check with a suitably qualified surveyor that your plans are sound.

In practice, a tub should be sited where it is easy and convenient to use; it can be positioned near a patio seating or lounging area or even sited on a roof garden or balcony provided the weight can be safely supported. In colder climates it may be more sensible to position your hot tub or spa in a summer house, pagoda or other covered structure. It is possible to create a summer house effect around an outdoor tub by surrounding it with bamboo blinds and a pergola structure with a glass roof. If you have the space and your budget will stand it, a changing area and shower facilities close by will be appreciated.

Avoid siting your tub or spa near or under deciduous trees where the leaves will cause a nuisance in autumn, and make sure the site receives plenty of sun. Although a heated tub can be used in all weathers, a chilly or windy corner will never make it seem particularly inviting. If winds are a problem, use screens made of bamboo, trellis or evergreen shrubs.

As well as providing shelter, a pergola is a useful place to rig up lights for after-dark bathing. Underwater lights should be the 12-volt, low-wattage type (see pp. 142-3). If you want colored lights then the blues, yellows and oranges tend to look better than the reds or greens. In general, keep colored lighting to a minimum to avoid a carnivallike appearance.

– INSTALLATION AND MATERIALS –

Hot tubs are not difficult to install – a building permit from your zoning board and access to safe water and electricity are all you need. Many models are attractive enough to stand above ground,

The hot tub looks best when integrated into a garden or patio design using plants and natural materials. Here, woven screens and bold-leaved plants provide an attractive setting.

HOW IT WORKS

The water in a hot tub is circulated and recycled by a centrifugal pump that sucks water out at the bottom and forces it through a filtration system and heater and returns it at the top. The system is usually boosted with hydro jets or an air blower (or both) to produce a strong jet of moving water or a bubble action. A filter keeps the water clean.

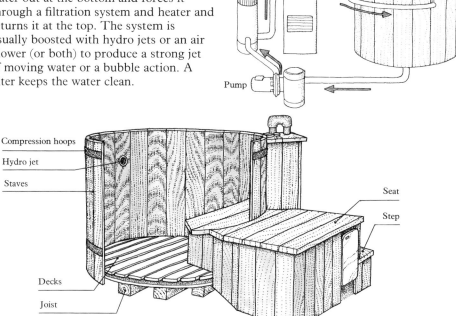

ABOVE *A wooden deck is useful for landscaping a hot tub into the garden as here, where the deck, in stepped scaffolding, hides the sides of the tub.*

LEFT *Wood is the obvious setting for a wooden hot tub and this design shows off its versatility with a combination of deck, pergola and wooden shelving surround for plants.*

which keeps costs down and makes them more portable if you move. Spas, however, do not have quite the attraction of a wooden tub since fiberglass can never rival wood for texture, warmth and softness, but set at ground level with a wooden deck overlapping the edges and fine plants around the perimeter, they make a most acceptable alternative.

A typical wooden tub has a round base, straight sides and is made of unstained redwood, but other shapes and woods are available. Redwood is most often used because it resists rot well, is not prone to splintering and swells easily when wet, keeping the tub watertight without the need to nail or glue the staves. Properly maintained, it should last as long as 15 years, but redwood is not particularly resistant to damage from caustic chemicals. Slightly more resistant is cedar, but it is not quite as long lasting. Oak, although far more costly, is very durable, while teak, the most expensive wood of all, is most resistant to decay. The price of wood can vary according to availability and location, so do shop around for the best price. Make sure you buy heart-wood only, since other cuts of wood are likely to leak or splinter.

Accessories

The pumping, heating and filtration systems essential for a hot tub or spa must be compatible if they are to work properly. It is therefore advisable to obtain all your components from one reputable hot tub center or to buy a ready-made model with all systems installed. Many tubs and spas are available in kit form and will include a compatible pump, filter, heater and hydro jet system, as well as a length of hose, drains and other necessary plumbing accessories. Optional extras are blowers to create a bubble effect, insulated covers to retain the heat when the tub is not in use, water testers, steps and platforms.

– PLANTS AND SURROUNDS –

It is important to choose plants that are going to look good when you are sitting in the tub or spa as well as when viewing it from the outside. The surrounding area can be softened by adding pots and baskets of dramatic architectural plants with interesting or large-leaf foliage such as *Phormium, Cordyline, Peltiphyllum,* ferns, palms and bamboos – all of which will thrive in the moist warm atmosphere around a tub or spa. Try also to include a few sweet-smelling herbs such as lemon balm and rosemary, climbers such as honeysuckle and climbing roses for a pergola, and flowers such as geraniums and lavender for tubs and pots scattered around the edges.

The tub's immediate surrounds should provide a dry, comfortable surface and be chosen to harmonize with the house and garden: paving, brick blocks or a wooden deck, for example. Do not use natural stone, such as fieldstone, since it tends to be too slippery and potentially dangerous when wet.

Health and safety with tubs and spas

It is absolutely essential that not only the fabric of your tub or spa is carefully maintained but that the water should be kept scrupulously clean and healthy. Pay strict regard to the following points and use the necessary chemicals carefully, following the printed instructions.

☐ Always shower before getting into the water to ensure that it stays clean.
☐ Run the filtration system for at least one hour per person using it per day.
☐ Shock-treat the water with chemicals as recommended.
☐ Never allow children to use it unattended.
☐ Do not use glassware in or near the tub or spa.
☐ Never allow animals into the water.
☐ Make sure the water is covered with a strong insulating cover to retain heat and prevent children or animals falling in when unattended.

HOT TUB SHAPES

The choice of hot tub shapes is really quite wide, as can be seen here. If space is limited, then a simple compact square or circular tub is probably best. With more space available, however, consider installing a free-form, stretched double rectangle or keyhole shape hot tub, depending on the style of the setting.

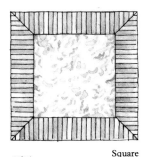
Square

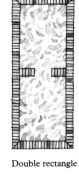
Double rectangle

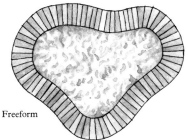
Freeform

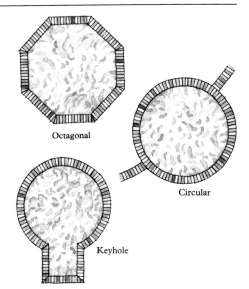
Octagonal

Keyhole

Circular

SWIMMING & SPLASH POOLS

◆

Swimming pools are the most difficult water feature to integrate successfully into a garden. By their very nature they have to be large and, therefore, dominating, yet readily accessible from the house both for convenience and for the provision of electricity, drainage, shower and changing facilities.

– SITING A POOL –

The perfect pool site should be free from strong cross-winds, soil and falling leaves – a particular problem in autumn – as well as having sufficient space around the pool itself to distance it from the rest of the garden, provide somewhere to sit and relax and, ideally, a place to change and shower.

An important point to bear in mind when considering installing a pool is that the water must be kept scrupulously clean. This entails running an effective pump and filtration system as well as the regular testing and treatment of the water. To accommodate the hardware necessary for this, the pool site should be large enough for the inclusion of a shed, cabin or summerhouse, sturdily con-structed of brick or lumber to match the surrounds. If it is sufficiently large, changing and shower facilities can also be included in this one structure. The building can be tucked behind the pool and disguised by planting trees and shrubs to provide attractive cover.

– INTEGRATING A POOL –

It is possible to incorporate a swimming pool attractively into the general design of your garden if you follow the natural contours of the site and surrounding area and plan it accordingly. You will find that the choice of shape and position are far more crucial to success than size – a small garden can take a large pool as a major feature if it is well thought out and sensitively installed.

INSTALLATION

Whatever size swimming pool you are planning to install, it is important to allow sufficient space for essential service equipment. Apart from a wide, flat area round the pool itself, you will have to install a pump, filter and heating equipment nearby, preferably housed together in a single shelter, shed or other building.

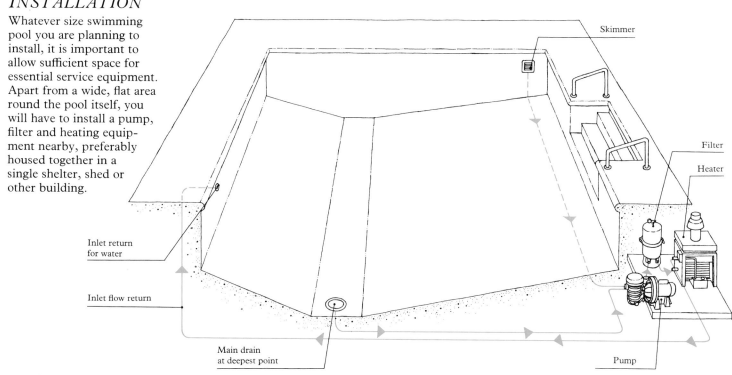

Skimmer

Filter

Heater

Inlet return for water

Inlet flow return

Main drain at deepest point

Pump

To decide the style and shape of pool that best suits your garden, draw the exact shape of your house and garden to scale on a piece of graph paper and experiment with plotting different size and shape pools. Look for forms that have some relationship to the existing architecture or to your garden shape, aiming for a good geometric balance. Squares and circles, for example, fit well together, and a circular pool in a small square garden or a kidney-shaped design in a rectangular plot always works well. Symmetrical shapes, such as squares and rectangles, look better set asymmetrically within the shape of the garden. Always run the length of the pool across the site so that you will not see a great expanse of water (the opposite principle to ornamental pools). The type of plan you can draw can be seen on pp. 124-5.

While the rectangle is the best shape for swimmers, a curved or kidney-shaped pool is often easier to fit successfully into an irregular plot or mold into the contours of a hilly landscape. If you are lucky enough to have a sloping site, you will find that even large pools can be set into the side of the slope and virtually disguised by avoiding the flat expanse of water inevitable with a level site. If, however, the pool is intended for young children to use as well, it is essential to provide a shallow end, a safety ledge running right round the sides of the pool, and gently wide steps.

The best type of pool construction is concrete sprayed onto a steel frame and then faced with tiles, and is carried out by

This is an excellent example of how a family swimming pool can be integrated with adjacent ornamental or wildlife ponds. The pools are separated by paving with raised flower beds so that the plants are prevented from polluting the swimming pool.

professional installers. Tile color is an important consideration – greens and browns tend to help the pool blend in with the rest of the garden while whites and blues will make more of a feature of the water itself. A less expensive option is a preformed steel-frame pool, available in a wide range of shapes and sizes, covered with a heavy-duty butyl liner.

Another way of integrating a swimming pool into the garden is to combine it with an ornamental water feature, provided that you remember that you cannot grow plants or keep fish because of the risk of chlorine or salination leaking through. You can, however, create water-falls, cascades and fountains in linked pools, or even build an island in the ornamental pool to grow plants as long as they have no contact with the water.

– SPLASH POOLS –

A splash pool can be good fun for adults and children, either used as part of a full-sized swimming pool or on its own where a large pool would be impracticable. The minimum size should be approximately $3 \times 4m/10 \times 13ft$ with a depth of about 90cm/36in.

As part of a larger swimming pool, a splash pool can share all the same heating and filtration facilities. From a design

An informal curved swimming pool such as this tends to be easy to landscape successfully. Paving slabs, graduating to an area of rough boulders, surround the swimming pool before merging into the planted area.

point of view, too, a splash pool is best incorporated into the main pool rather than installed nearby in isolation. Interlocking circles, curves, squares or rectangles can be used and they will help to avoid the public swimming pool atmosphere. If you do wish to install a children's splash pool on its own, site it within view of the kitchen or living room windows, and cover it with a locking wooden lid when it is not in use.

INTEGRATING SPLASH POOLS

If your garden is small, or the site dictates, a splash pool can be used as a separate garden feature. A good idea, however, is to integrate a splash pool and swimming pool. In this way, both pools can share the same pump and filtration system, and the two can be further integrated by using a common surface surround, such as brick, tiles or sandstone.

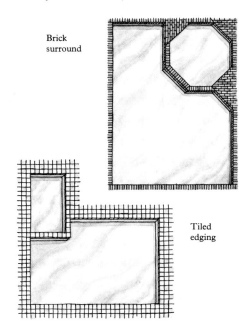

Brick surround

Tiled edging

Natural sandstone

Dense planting around the poolside looks attractive and acts as a windbreak. It should, however, be well contained to prevent soil blowing into the water. Use trees or a pergola to add height.

– POOL SURROUNDS –

The surrounding pool surface should be even, nonslip, easy to clean, stable for garden furniture and be in harmony with the rest of the garden. It should also slope gently back from the edge of the pool so that rain water does not wash into it. Depending on the style of the house, you can choose from tiles, bricks, paving and wood – all perform equally well, although wood is warmest underfoot. It is also a good surface when used in conjunction with a hot tub (see pp. 82-5) and should be scrubbed, sanded, preserved and stained to provide a hard-wearing, attractive, nonsplinter finish. Use hardwoods such as teak, oroko and oak. Paved and brick surfaces can be arranged in herringbone or basketweave patterns to offset the sometimes smooth blandness of the pool's surface (see pp. 70-5). If you are considering using tiles make sure they have a nonslip surface.

In all cases you must have a fence around your pool, even if you do not have any children, and, again, the materials you use will depend on the style of the rest of the garden. Choose from brick

POOL SURROUNDS

Swimming pool surrounds can be as imaginative as those for ornamental pools – if you have both features, use the surround to link the two. A basketweave pattern of mellow brick (below), rough stones and wood softened by creeping plants (bottom), and a pattern of edging tiles with raised beds (right) are alternative ways of integrating pool areas.

walls, pierced concrete blocks, trellis, bamboo screens and reed panels or grow tall hedges of, for example, yew.

Relandscaping the garden after the pool has been installed usually consists of softening the surrounds to make the pool look more natural. The excavated soil is always useful for providing a change in level, but should be redistributed into a gentle mound rather than left in one large pile. Remember to leave easy access to the pool itself and to make sure that surrounding flower beds are clearly defined, to prevent earth being washed into the pool area. Plants do much to add interest and large tubs and containers of bright annuals and shrubs will help to distract the eye from the hard lines of the pool itself.

– Raised Pools –

If a difficult site or finance preclude the installation of a sunken pool, a prefabricated, above-ground pool can be added to the garden instead. If care is taken, its impact on the garden can be minimized by incorporating it into a natural slope or building up the sides with wooden decking. This can be extended to include further decked areas for sunbathing, sitting and eating, softened with tubs of trees, annuals, shrubs and bamboos.

Raised pools are usually circular or oval in shape to withstand the pressure of water – without the support of surrounding soil, corners tend to weaken and split. They have a maximum diameter of about 7.3m/24ft and depth of 1.2m/4ft. Because they are considered to be portable, they do not usually need a building permit but it is advisable to check with your zoning board before installing one.

LANDSCAPING A NATURAL POOL

A sloping site offers excellent opportunities for landscaping a large swimming pool successfully into the garden. A level garden (right) featured a fine craggy outcrop which made the perfect backdrop of height and interest to a lagoon-style pool. The more formal pool (below right) has been built into the natural contours of a gradient.

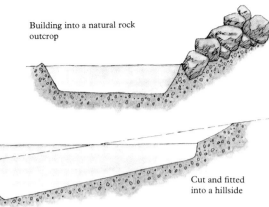

Building into a natural rock outcrop

Cut and fitted into a hillside

– Pool Maintenance –

Swimming and splash pools need vigilant and constant maintenance if the water is to remain clean and healthy. A filter is essential and should recycle the water about every eight hours, removing any dirt particles and returning clean water to the pool. General health of the water is maintained using chemicals and regular testing and treatment (see pp. 148-51). Pool covers are often more trouble than they are worth in warm climates, because they are difficult to roll and unroll and save a few degrees only of heat. They are, however, essential in cold weather and if you have young children (see pp. 152-3).

– Water Indoors –

Water features need not be restricted to the garden; they can make a splendid focal point indoors as part of a covered swimming pool complex or conservatory or anywhere that has large areas of glass to let in plenty of light, such as a summer house. Water without natural light looks gloomy and unattractive, a problem not completely relieved by the addition of artificial light, which tends to make the water seem overly theatrical.

To avoid an hotel or office lobby atmosphere, keep the design of your indoor water feature simple, and choose materials that relate in some way to the surrounding area – for example, tiles, brick, glass or clear fiberglass. It can be as large or small as space permits – a simple water sculpture adding movement and interest to an indoor swimming pool, or a large pool with waterfalls in a plant-dominated conservatory.

A more unusual idea is to link an indoor room with the patio area using water. Build a small bridge across the doorway with a stretch of water either side and tile, brick or deck the floor to match the patio. You will generally find that a formal-shaped pool (square, rectangular or hexagonal) fits better into a small or medium-sized room where it can be built into a corner and takes up less space. But do not be frightened to experiment with other shapes, such as classic fan- and seashell-shaped pools.

If you are contemplating installing a large water feature, you must have a structural survey carried out to see if there are any likely problems. Like outdoor pools, any indoor pool must have drainage facilities so that cleaning and maintenance can be carried out.

A naturally lit indoor pool area provides an excellent opportunity to grow some of the more tender aquatic plants, but many of the smaller varieties recommended for outdoor ponds and pools are equally suitable for indoor planting as well. Because of the warm, sheltered conditions, there is a danger of plants proliferating and overcrowding the available space, so avoid growing too many vigorous types and trim back regularly. Aim for a good balance of leaf shape and size with some spectacular blooming plants for special interest. The showy spoon-flower (*Xanthosoma nigrum*), for example, has bright yellow, arumlike flowers on purple stems and taro (*Colocasia antiquorum*) has magnificent large, green/purple leaves, again with yellow flowers. Both of these plants will make a fine contrast with a low-growing plant, such as the pale green water lettuce (*Pistia stratiotes*) or the elegant, slender stems of umbrella grass (*Cyperus alternifolius*), sugar cane (*Saccharum officinarum*) or even rice (*Oryza sativa*).

The indoor water garden is an ideal place for growing exotic water flowers, too, and, if you have a small pool only, it is worth including some dwarf varieties. It is difficult to do better than the water hyacinth (*Eichhornia speciosa*), for example, for providing a mass of lovely blooms or one of the tropical water lilies. Look also at the arum lily (*Zantedeschia aethiopica*), the huge white or pink lotus blooms of *Nelumbo nucifera* or the *Nymphaea lotus*, which blooms at night.

Large areas of glass and plenty of foliage plants help to integrate an indoor pool with the garden beyond without losing any of the advantages of warmth and shelter.

MAKING A FEATURE

An attractive alternative to a pool is to sink a water reservoir and pump under the floor and have a small fountain running continuously over a bed of pebbles set flush with the floor.

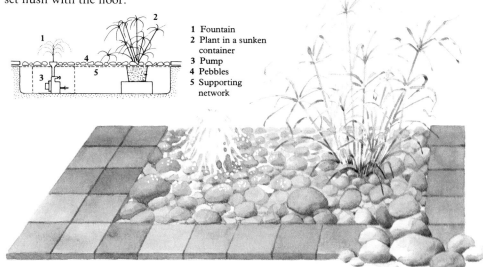

1 Fountain
2 Plant in a sunken container
3 Pump
4 Pebbles
5 Supporting network

STOCKING THE WATER GARDEN

What you need to know to plan an effective planting design; large- and small-leaved waterside plants, their height, spread and flower color; moisture-loving plants, ideal for the patio water garden; ferns, reeds and rushes, grasses and sedges; water lilies, to cover the surface of the water; oxygenators, to keep the water healthy; trees and shrubs, to provide the perfect backdrop; tender plants, for the indoor or subtropical water garden

WHEN YOU BEGIN planning a planting design for your water garden, consider first the lush, bold, large-leaved species that enhance the quality of the water itself – plants that are dramatic for their form, and the shape and color of their foliage, rather than the brightness of their blooms.

Many of the bolder water plants are special species that thrive in the moist soil at the water's edge. Those with large, strongly-shaped leaves look better planted individually and not mixed with other species; in general, it is better to select just a few different plants than try to cram in as many species as possible. Smaller-leaved waterside plants can be effective, too, but because each plant's spread tends to be small, they should be planted in clumps of a single species.

Many waterside plants – including rushes, reeds and some grasses and ferns – will grow in the shallows with their roots and part of their stems submerged in water. Known to botanists as 'emergent' plants, they can make a dramatic display in small ponds where their leaves and blooms make a contrast with other, background plants.

You will, of course, want to include some plants that float on the water's surface in your final plan. These plants, which form a mat of leaves supporting their weight, include the renowned and beautiful water lily, *Nymphaea,* which has many varieties and cultivars. Water lilies quickly cover the water's surface with their round green pads and have larger and more distinctive blooms than

ABOVE *The damp conditions surrounding pools and streams create an excellent environment for growing unusual plants, such as* Lysichitum americanum, *which flowers in the spring and should be planted in either shallow water or in boggy ground in a sunny position.*

LEFT *Mass planting of a single species, such as* Buphthalmum speciosum, *tends to look more effective than a tightly packed mixture of different types. Note the effect of a single color against a background of different greens, too.*

many land plants. It is no surprise that the Impressionist Claude Monet, with his eye for color and light effects, was inspired in his old age to paint the ever-changing magic of his water garden at Giverny near Paris, continuing to capture the dazzling reflections made by the water lilies even as his eyesight failed.

True floating plants, to the botanist, are those which, unlike the water lilies, do not root in the soil at the pond bottom. They have an ability to multiply very rapidly and need careful control in small ponds where they can cover the whole surface, trapping air and altering the natural balance of the pond with disastrous results. Also invasive, but mainly underwater and sometimes rooted, are the oxygenating plants, which are very important in maintaining a healthy pond.

An essential part of the water garden planting design are shrubs and trees, not only for their height and massed effect, but for the lovely reflections they make on the water's surface, and also because their own leaves reflect light onto the water. Because they tend to be large and permanent features, they need very careful thought before planting – in particular, take account of their mature size, leaf drop and root systems. This does not mean that any existing trees should be removed if they are not included on pp. 119-21, for the selection there is confined to species particularly suited to moist situations and is not meant to be definitive. Other trees and shrubs will be more suitable for your own garden, or will be chosen for their autumn color, or be-

Water lilies can be prolific growers and are best cultivated in wire baskets supported on the pool bottom so that you can lift them easily for pruning, as required.

cause they attract wildlife. But if, for reasons of scale, the right choice is difficult, consider growing the tree in a pot to restrict its growth.

– ELEMENTS OF GOOD PLANTING –

For a planting plan to work successfully, it should be devised as a whole rather than patched together piecemeal as the garden develops. This will enable you to judge the best positions for key plants, an obvious but often forgotten rule. You will need to decide the main viewpoint, whether it is from the house, from a patio, or perhaps from an approach to the pool.

Large-leaved plants, taller irises and reeds should be planted to the rear of the pond, with smaller ones, such as primulas, forget-me-nots, pontederias and frogbit, to the fore. Remember that some larger plants will spread – especially the large-leaved species such as *Gunnera*, *Ligularia* and *Peltiphyllum* – so plant them slightly back from the water's edge, giving them space to spread out over it.

Mature size and growth patterns must also be considered, as a small plant that neither spreads nor grows tall will be lost in a large pond, while a small pool will be swamped by large-leaved or invasive species. It is a surprisingly common mistake to find a water feature disappearing under a mountain of water lilies, or a pond that has to be drained and cleared of invasive reeds.

Groupings of plants within the pond area need as careful consideration as those of pond-side ones: water lilies look better in clusters set to one side, rather

The formal bog garden is usually contained by brick or stone adjoining a formal pool and filled with moist soil. The wonderful variety of bog and waterside plants allows a fine contrast of different leaf shapes and colors.

than in the center of a pool, and reeds or rushes are better in two or three large clumps than lots of smaller ones.

The overall choice of plants should have a good balance of shape and color without mixing too many species or neglecting to have something of interest for every season. Flowering periods can often be staggered from early spring to autumn and even winter, while evergreen shrubs and catkin-bearing trees are useful in winter when there is not much happening in the water garden.

Certain combinations of plants do work extremely well: for example, tall linear reeds with large-leaved *Peltiphyllum* and *Ligularia*; primula and iris; or primulas with hostas and *Rodgersia*. But the very big-leaved plants such as *Petasites* should stand alone as they will quickly overtake smaller plants.

A single dramatic species of plant often looks more effective in a small pool than several smaller ones. Here, lovely white iris dominate a small, round formal pool with stunning results.

Some color combinations work better than others, too; try planting blues, creams, whites and yellows together, or a combination of pinks, purples, blues and magentas. Avoid orange/blue, red/yellow or blue/red combinations as these tend to clash or look too harsh.

– PLANTS AND WATER FEATURES –

To prevent a static planting design and to keep a water feature looking at its best all year round, it is a good idea to plant many of your plants in pots or baskets which are then submerged (see pp. 144-5). The plants can then be moved around or exchanged for different ones once they are past their prime. This

LEFT *Planting beds enclosed by paving or retaining walls look good bordering more formal pools, and they also help to contain plants likely to be rampant growers.*

RIGHT *Large areas surrounding informal pools need careful planning and maintenance if one or two species are not to be allowed to dominate. Remember to keep tall plants to the back and to mix only the softer shades of color.*

treatment is also perfect for half-hardy species, such as the shapely arum lily, *Zantedeschia aethiopica,* which will produce lush, abundant foliage if its pot is submerged in water during the summer months, but will appreciate being removed to a greenhouse and kept fairly dry during colder months.

Other architectural water plants – reeds, iris, early-flowering marsh marigolds, *Pontederia* and papyrus – can look good placed at the foot of a fountain or other water feature so that they form part of a flexible design. Moisture-loving species such as hostas, *Peltiphyllum* and *Ligularia* can also be planted in pots and stood near water features. In this case, the pots should not be submerged in water, as these species do not like to be waterlogged.

Waterfalls, streams and bubble fountains with rocks and stones at the sides, or watercourses with very shallow water, often present problems for planting. However, cracks can be left between stones, or rock pockets filled with earth, to support small ivies, creeping Jenny (*Lysimachia nummularia*) and small ferns such as the hart's tongue fern (*Phyllitis scolopendrium*). These plants are specially adapted to derive moisture from cracks in rock and stone in their natural habitat.

Another way of softening rocks and stones at the base of fountains and other features is to plant ornamental grasses, mosses or lichens. The latter two, however, can be difficult to establish.

Many formal pools will not have a moist edge for planting as they are made of concrete or butyl liners. This can be overcome by making deep excavations round the pool sides and backfilling with peat and compost before introducing water plants. An alternative is to use pots, using the same type of pot and plants both in and out of the water, to make a visual link between the two areas.

– SITUATION AND SOIL –

As you will notice from the catalog of plants that follows, most water plants are easy to please as far as sun and soil are concerned, providing the ground is moist and the situation not too shady. Very few species will thrive in complete shade, even the shade-lovers such as hostas, primulas, ferns and *Rodgersia* which need some dappled light to flourish. Others, like the large-leaved plants (*Gunnera* and *Rheum*) and most of the flowering varieties, need a certain amount of sunlight (an average of 4 to 5 hours per day) to be at their best.

Because the majority of waterside and pond plants are prolific growers, they are greedy feeders and it will help both growth and health if you can use the best quality soil and add plenty of compost enriched with peat or bonemeal.

Key to plant entries, pp. 100-22
In the following entries: H = height of plant above soil or water level; S = spread; and D = water depth required for pond plants.

WATERSIDE PLANTS

To help you in your choice of pond- or stream-side plants, they have been grouped according to form and/or situation within the following categories: *Large-leaved plants*; *Small-leaved plants*; *Moisture-loving plants*; *Ferns*; *Reeds and rushes*; *Grasses and sedges*. Flowering species have been shown in flower and are sometimes shown thus grouped together although they do not all necessarily bloom at the same time. Many waterside plants are suitable for bog gardens, and this has been noted.

LARGE-LEAVED WATERSIDE PLANTS

Many of the plants that grow on the shores of ponds and streams have large, boldly shaped leaves and fast growth rates. Where space is limited, many of them will make good specimen plants.

Each plant's preference for situation and soil is indicated; those that prefer moist as opposed to wet soil should be planted further from the water's edge and the soil should be enriched with humus or moisture-retaining peat.

BRUNNERA *macrophylla*

H 50cm/20in S 1m/3ft 3in

A hardy plant that will survive in dry conditions, but if given moisture will make huge, heart-shaped leaves with sprays of tiny blue flowers rising above them. This plant prefers shade, but in moist conditions will grow happily in full sun. Do not plant directly at the water's edge; it grows best in moist woodland near or around a bog garden.

CARDIOCRINUM *giganteum*

H 1.8-3m/6-9ft S 90cm/36in

This, the largest flowering plant in the lily family, has a slightly tropical appearance and looks particularly good planted in a group, the bold strap-shaped leaves creating an almost exotic effect. In sum-mer it produces large trumpet-shaped flowers to 25cm/10in long and, later, large seed cases. A hardy plant, it is happiest in partial shade and likes very deep (90cm/36in) humus-enriched soil, but does not like the soil too moist, so ensure good drainage around the bulbs to prevent rotting. The plant takes about 6 years to flower and dies after flowering.

GUNNERA *manicata*

H 2-4m/6ft 6in-13ft S 3-4.5m/10-15ft

A hardy perennial, *G. manicata* is the largest-leaved plant that can be grown under garden conditions. Its natural habitat is on the lower slopes of the Andes, where it is fed by melting snows. The leaves can be up to 4m/13ft across, equaling the plant's height. It enjoys the deep mud at the side of a large pond or lake and does not mind shade. In cold climates it should be covered over during severe winter months; alternatively, cut off the leaves in autumn and wrap them over the crown of the plant.

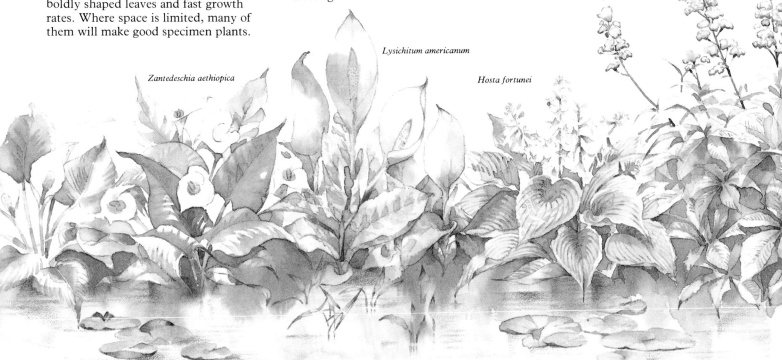

Rodgersia pinnata

Lysichitum americanum

Hosta fortunei

Zantedeschia aethiopica

G. scabra

H to 1.8m/6ft	S 2-3m/6ft 6in-10ft

This variety has slightly smaller leaves and a more spreading habit than *G. manicata,* and is also hardier, tolerating colder conditions and more exposed planting sites. However, treat *G. scabra* in the same way, protecting it well against frosts and cold winds in winter.

HERACLEUM mantegazzianum

GIANT HOGWEED

H 1.8-3.6m/6-12ft	S 1.2m/4ft

Originally from the Caucasus, this giant short-lived perennial flourishes in rich, moist soil and will spread rapidly. The flat white flowerheads in summer can be up to 60cm/24in across on thick, hollow stems. The sap is very poisonous and even the hairy stems can cause blistering. The flowers should be removed before the seeds ripen, for this plant soon becomes invasive.

HOSTA fortunei

PLANTAIN LILY

H 60cm/24in	S 40cm/16in

Often classified under the genus name *Funkia,* this hardy herbaceous perennial is from China. Its deeply veined gray-green leaves are sufficient to give the plant its own character, but the blue-lilac flowers on erect spikes with small hanging bells in midsummer are stunning. Although it is rather susceptible to slugs, *H. fortunei* is a valuable asset to the gardener seeking a 'form-loving' plant. It is happiest in damp, shady conditions in soil enriched with peat or humus.

H. sieboldiana 'Elegans'

H to 90cm/36in	S 60cm/24in

Of all the hostas, this one has the largest leaves. Grown from seed, this hardy plant will have slight variation in depth of leaf color. The light gray-green and more blue leaves look fantastic set in groups by the water's edge. The flowers, which appear in midsummer, are a very pale lilac, set in rather stumpy clumps standing just above the mounds of leaves.

H. ventricosa

H 60cm/24in	S 40cm/16in

The finest green-leaved hosta, with broad, rich, dark heart-shaped leaves, evenly veined. It does well in heavy shade.

Cardiocrinum giganteum

Petasites japonicus

Ligularia clivorum 'Desdemona'

Gunnera manicata

LIGULARIA clivorum 'Desdemona'

H 1.2m/4ft   S 1m/3ft 3in

This hardy hybrid has purple coloring on the underside of its large, beautiful heart-shaped leaves – the perfect complement to the large flowerheads, 1.5m/5ft tall, carrying up to 20 orange daisylike flowers, that appear in late summer and attract plenty of bees and butterflies. It is not fussy about soil type as long as the soil is moist and well-fed with humus. It needs shelter from strong sunlight and wind.

L. dentata 'Gregynog Gold'

H 1-1.2m/3ft 3in-4ft   S 1m/3ft 3in

Grown in large clumps, this is a particularly beautiful flowering species, attracting butterflies with its conical spires of large bright yellow daisylike flowers in late summer. Useful for smaller ponds.

L. przewalskii

H 1.2m/4ft   S 1m/3ft 3in

This species, grown in clumps, is similar to *L. stenocephala* with its erect spikes of lemon-yellow flowers.

L. stenocephala 'The Rocket'

H to 1.5m/5ft   S 1m/3ft 3in

This fine cut-leaf cultivar has the most handsome black flower stems opening to lemon-yellow flowerheads on erect spikes, 1.5m/5ft tall. Each spike carries up to 50 flowers, and blooms before both 'Desdemona' and 'Gregynog Gold'.

LYSICHITUM americanum

SKUNK CABBAGE

H 1.2m/4ft   S 60cm/24in

Originating from the peat marshes of central California, this hardy herbaceous perennial thrives in sun in muddy and boggy situations where its roots can penetrate 1.2-1.8m/4-6ft deep. Although slow to establish itself, it is a dramatic plant, with large bright yellow arumlike flowers in early spring followed by giant banana-shaped leaves that appear out of the mud and grow to 1.5m/5ft. The flowers give off a strange scent, particularly on a warm day, giving the plant its common name.

PELTIPHYLLUM peltatum

H 1.5m/5ft   S indefinite

This unusual hardy plant has beautiful large peltate-shaped, parasollike leaves standing 90cm/36in tall. It has spreading thick rhizomes which will form a thick mat over a stream or pond bank. In early summer, slim hairy stems appear and develop into flat heads of pale pink flowers; the leaves follow after, reaching 35cm/14in across, and turning a coppery red in autumn, before being cut down by early frost. The plant will tolerate full sun, but grows best in some shade and it prefers wet soil.

PETASITES japonicus

JAPANESE BUTTERBUR

H 25cm/10in   S 2m/6ft 6in or more

This creeping hardy herbaceous perennial can be found growing wild along rivers and streams in Japan and Europe together with *Petasites hybridus*. The rufflike yellow flowers appear in early spring and are much treasured by flower arrangers. Their high nectar content makes them popular with bees, and the plant is ideal for wild gardens. An invaluable plant for cool shady sites where large-leaved ground cover is required, *P. japonicus* needs moist but not necessarily rich soil nor deep planting.

RHEUM palmatum

H 1.8m/6ft   S 1.8m/6ft

This ornamental rhubarb is an eye-catching hardy perennial from the high rocky streams of China. It produces giant overlapping bright green leaves up to 90cm/36in across, and its flowers are borne in a panicle. It grows in sun or shade and likes a damp compost-enriched soil with its roots out of water. The hybrid *R.p.* 'Purpureum' has a finer cut leaf with red-purple undersides flowering with a tall pink flower in early summer. This plant is especially good for areas where a large leaf is needed to contrast with irises or primulas.

RODGERSIA pinnata

H 1m/3ft 3in   S 80cm/30in

This hardy perennial takes a year or two to become established but is most rewarding with soft white, pink or red fluffy flowers in large panicles, over 90cm/36in tall, in late spring and deeply cut distinctive leaves. Like the rest of its genus, it thrives in moist soil and does not like full sun. Grow in the shade of a tree close to the water's edge, perhaps next to irises.

R. tabularis

H 60cm/24in   S 50cm/20in

This hardy round-leaved perennial is slow to develop. Its soft fluffy white flowers are fairly insignificant but the rounded apple-green leaves have one of the most beautiful greens of any plant. It requires a position sheltered from hot sun and drying winds, with damp woodland soil.

ZANTEDESCHIA aethiopica

ARUM LILY

H 90cm/36in   S 90cm/36in

This wild South African lily, already well known, can be grown both in the water (in wire baskets) or as a waterside plant. Its tropical appearance, with its spectacular white flowers, makes it ideal for city gardens. It is not suitable for very cold climates and does not tolerate frost, and should be lifted and kept in a frost-free greenhouse during winter. In warmer climates it grows at the edge of ponds to provide continuous summer flowering.

SMALL-LEAVED WATERSIDE PLANTS

The less dramatic, small-leaved waterside plants are rewarding not only for their fast growth but also for the beauty of their flowers – an added pleasure when the plant can be seen reflected in water. Planting them in groups will ensure strength and form in your overall water garden design, particularly important with large ponds where one or two small-leaved plants would be rather lost, however beautiful.

Most of the plants here tolerate wet soil and some even prefer their roots submerged in water; however, most require a sunny situation.

CALLA *palustris*

BOG ARUM

H 10cm/4in   S over several meters

This hardy plant, a native of Canada and north-east USA, anchors itself at the waterside and floats out over the surface, forming large mats of small, shiny heart-shaped leaves with white arumlike flowers in early summer, or after the second year, in late spring. As its common name indicates, it is a good plant for bog gardens; it is impartial to soil but requires sun. It is a useful plant for softening the edges of ponds.

CALTHA *palustris*

MARSH MARIGOLD

H 30cm/12in   S 30cm/12in

Also familiarly known as the king cup, this hardy plant, with its attractive, heart-shaped leaves, is common throughout Europe, North America and Asia. It flowers early in spring and looks at its best planted in large groups to allow its fine flowers, like very large buttercups, to radiate their warm yellow color. It prefers a wet rich soil and sun. *C.p. pleno*, the double-flowered variety, is more compact and better suited to small urban ponds, where its leaves make good ground cover. 'Alba' is a white form that prefers a slightly drier situation.

GEUM *rivale*

WATER AVENS

H 60cm/24in   S 50cm/20in

A native of Europe and America, this hardy spreading plant is also good for growing in damp soil, in sun or shade. Its insignificant soft orange flowers stand 30cm/12in above clusters of green divided leaves on hairy red stems. *G. × borisii* makes good ground cover, producing neat clumps of dark green leaves and bright orange-red flowers in early summer. It will also thrive well in a border but requires good mulching with well-rotted manure or compost. *Geum* is best planted in large groups to give maximum color impact, and they will also combine well with primulas and hostas.

IRIS *kaempferi*

JAPANESE IRIS

H 90cm/36in   S 45cm/18in

Most species of iris are hardy and require little attention except being kept free of invasive plants and grasses. This, the iris seen in traditional pictures of Japanese gardens, is an exotic-looking plant with predominant, enlarged falls on its purple flowers in midsummer, and has slender deciduous foliage. The colors of its cultivars range from white through pink and lavender to violet. It likes a wet, rich soil and sun.

Iris kaempferi

Geum rivale

Caltha palustris

Calla palustris

I. laevigata

WATER IRIS

H 45-60cm/18-24in   S 45cm/18in

This plant has lavender blue flowers, three to a stem, in early summer, and is an excellent plant for bog gardens. It grows best in water 5-13cm/2-5in deep, but will tolerate deeper water than *I. kaempferi*, and grows well planted in wet mud at the side of a pond in sun. *I.l.* 'Alba' is the white form and is not as vigorous. *I.l.* 'Variegata' has light blue flowers and striped leaves.

I. pseudacorus

YELLOW FLAG

H 1-1.5m/3ft 3in-5ft   S 50cm/20in

Frequently seen growing along river banks from Europe to central Asia, the flag iris likes a boggy, sunny situation. Its light green leaves are shaped like long swords and often have a blue tinge.

MENTHA aquatica

WATER MINT

H 30cm/12in   S indefinite

The hardy water mint will thrive in shallow water, since it will live either on the water surface or in soil, and has bright green hairy leaves in shady situations, turning to purple in full sunlight. It has a distinctive minty smell and flavor and produces spiky pom-poms of bright blue flowers in late summer. It can be invasive.

Sagittaria japonica

MIMULUS guttatus

MONKEY MUSK

H 45cm/18in   S 30cm/12in

A superb, spreading, wet-loving plant with orchidlike spotted-yellow flowers in midsummer. Its leaves are midgreen and rounded. A self-seeding hardy annual, it tends to be rather rampant, making it ideal for masking unsightly edges of small pools. It likes a sunny situation in wet but well-drained soil, but will survive in drier conditions than most aquatics. There are many species in the genus *Mimulus*, some more erect in habit, suitable for bog gardens and also shade.

PONTEDERIA cordata

PICKEREL WEED

H 45-60cm/18-24in   S 15cm/6in

A fine hardy sun-loving plant found growing wild in shallow ponds and streams of central and eastern USA and eastern Canada. It has elegant, heart-shaped waxy light green leaves on long stalks, and attractive spikes of blue flowers in late summer. It looks good grown *en masse* to soften a pond edge. The less hardy *P. lanceolata* is larger, growing to 1.5m/5ft and has more elongated lancelike leaves. It grows best in water up to 12cm/5in deep.

Sagittaria sagittifolia

Pontederia cordata

SAGITTARIA japonica

ARROWHEAD

H 30cm/12in   S 20cm/8in

This hardy plant has larger arrow-shaped leaves than *S. sagittifolia* (see below) and the bonus of beautiful white double flowers up to 5cm/2in across. It should be planted in shallow water no more than 13cm/5in deep. The cultivar *S.s.* 'Flore Pleno' has particularly lovely flowerheads and blooms all summer.

S. sagittifolia

COMMON ARROWHEAD

H 45cm/18in   S 25cm/10in

A familiar sight among the shallows of ponds and rivers in Europe and Asia, the distinctive arrow-shaped leaves of this hardy herbaceous perennial rise above the water surface on long stems. It produces large white flowers with black centers.

Iris pseudacorus

MOISTURE-LOVING PLANTS

The plants included here can be grown away from the pond edge as they prefer a moist but well-drained soil, and are particularly useful in patio gardens or where the pond has a concrete or butyl lining – anywhere where there is no wet edge to the pond. Best results will be obtained by mulching well and by providing a humus-rich planting medium.

ARTEMISIA lactiflora

H 1.5m/5ft	S 1m/3ft 3in

This hardy plant is the exception to others in its family which prefer dry conditions. It grows naturally in moist meadows and stream valleys in western China. Its large, loose heads of creamy-white flowers late in summer are slightly scented.

ASTILBE × arendsii

H 50cm-1.5m/20in-5ft	S 20-90cm/8-36in

The astilbe family has many garden hybrids, most of which are collectively called *A. × arendsii*. They are invaluable plants for the water gardener as they are hardy and have a wide range of colors.

A. chinensis 'Pumila'

H 60cm/24in	S 60cm/24in

Plants of this genus require moist soil and prefer woodland conditions. *A.c.* 'Pumila' is a low growing form ideal for colorful ground cover in a very moist shady place. It has beautiful spikes of rose-colored flowers in midsummer.

EUPATORIUM purpureum

HEMP AGRIMONY

H 2-2.4m/6ft 6in-8ft	S 2m/6ft 6in

This impressive hardy damp-loving plant is found growing wild at the water's edge in south-east Canada and east USA. It

looks very striking with its large, purple-tinted stems and dark green, pointed leaves. It has fluffy mauve-pink flowers arranged in large flat flowerheads, up to 30cm/12in across, which bloom throughout the autumn.

FILIPENDULA palmata

H 1.2-1.5m/4-5ft	S 1m/3ft 3in

Sometimes also called *Spiraea*, *Filipendula* grows naturally in damp meadows. *F. palmata* is an elegant, hardy pond-side plant forming tall clumps with light green leaves topped by heads of tiny pink flowers.

F. ulmaria

MEADOWSWEET

H 30-75cm/12-30in	S 20cm/8in

The meadowsweet has two cultivars. *F.u.* 'Aurea' produces a mass of rich yellow foliage and creamy-white flowers in dense clusters in midsummer. It enjoys moist soil, making it ideal for the bog garden. It grows 30-40cm/12-16in tall. *F.u.* 'Variegata' has dark green leaves with yellow centers and grows to 75cm/30in.

HEMEROCALLIS

Astilbe sp.

DAY LILY

H 1m/3ft 3in	S 1m/3ft 3in

These tough, hardy plants are best suited to moist, sunny edges of ponds and lakes although they will grow quite happily in borders where they have sufficient moisture. Long grown in China, they have been hybridized into many colors and shades. Two ideal species for the water's edge are *H. flava* with its clear yellow lily-shaped scented flowers in early summer, and *H. fulva,* which has many hybrids. 'Rosea' is a soft coppery color and looks very good mixed with yellow- and pink-flowered plants of this species. All *Hemerocallis* are fairly prolific.

HOSTA fortunei 'Aurea'

H 50cm/20in	S 50cm/20in

This hosta, together with *H. lancifolia*, makes hardy ground cover to the water's edge without being too invasive. It has the brightest yellow leaves, almost butter yellow on first opening. It will tolerate full sun if given plenty of moisture.

H. lancifolia

H 45cm/18in   S 30-60cm/12-24in

This hardy hosta has dark green leaves, smaller than most of its genus. The flowers are a lovely dark lilac, excellent for flower arrangements. *H. lancifolia* requires some shade to be successful.

IRIS sibirica

H 1m/3ft 3in   S 1m/3ft 3in

This iris is a fine hardy plant for water-side gardens, but adapts to drier conditions. It grows best on the margin of a small lake or pond in any soil but prefers sun. It grows in clumps and will spread by seed. There are many different-colored forms but blue and to some extent white are the favorites.

LYSIMACHIA ciliata

H 1m/3ft 3in   S indefinite

A native of North America and Canada, this is a fine hardy spreading bog plant, useful for its late-flowering habit. It produces loose racemes with star-shaped yellow flowers in late summer. It needs sun and will tolerate drier conditions.

L. nummularia

CREEPING JENNY

H 2.5cm/1in   S indefinite

A hardy low ground-covering plant, prostrate in habit, creeping Jenny has yellow star-shaped flowers in mid-summer. It is extremely invasive.

L. punctata

H 1.5m/5ft   S 1m/3ft 3in

A yellow loosestrife, this is an ideal plant for damp, shady places, although it tends to become invasive if grown on the wet edges of streams or ponds. It produces branched clusters of yellow flowers in midsummer, and looks good planted in large groups against *Hemerocallis* or used as ground cover in wild gardens.

LYTHRUM salicaria

PURPLE LOOSESTRIFE

H 1.2-1.5m/4-5ft   S 1m/3ft 3in

Found in many countries of the world, *L. salicaria* is a quick-spreading hardy perennial with square stems. It has bright red-purple flowers on a spikelike raceme in midsummer. It will tolerate its roots in water and is superb for a bog garden. *L. virgata* is a smaller, similar, species.

Eupatorium purpureum

Lythrum salicaria

Filipendula palmata

Iris sibirica

Hosta lancifolia

POLYGONUM *bistorta* 'Superbum'

KNOTWEED

H 40cm/16in   S indefinite

This hybrid has soft mauve-pink flowers looking like small pokers, in early summer, and long, tall leaves. Although quite invasive, it can be easily checked. It is hardy, grows near water and tolerates fairly dense shade; where moisture is sufficient it will grow in full sun.

PRIMULA *florindae*

HIMALAYAN COWSLIP

H to 1m/3ft 3in   S 1m/3ft 3in

Originally from south-east Tibet, this tall primula has yellow flowers early to midsummer, and prefers to grow right at the water's edge where its red-colored roots seen underwater look particularly effective *en masse*. It grows in acid soil only and prefers half shade. In good conditions it will self-seed. All primulas enjoy a rich woodland soil and are hardy if short-lived perennials.

P. *helodoxa*

H to 1m/3ft 3in   S 1m/3ft 3in

This is an evergreen primula, a bit like *P. florindae* with darker yellow flowers from early to midsummer and thrives at the water's edge in acid soil and half shade.

P. *japonica*

H to 1m/3ft 3in   S 1m/3ft 3in

An easily grown, self-seeding variety which first flowers in late spring to early summer, with vibrant mauve-crimson flowerheads. It has broad, pale green crinkled leaves and requires an acid soil and, like other primulas of the candelabra type, adores slightly shady pool edges. The cultivar 'Postford's White' has white, rounded inflorescences with yellow eyes.

P. *pulverulenta*

H 20cm/8in   S 30cm/12in

A primula that adapts well to growing in moist and bog garden areas, with deep wine-colored flowers with purple eyes standing about 60cm/24in above the leaves. The flower stems have a speckled white appearance, giving the plant a distinctive look. It should be planted in large groups for greatest color impact.

TROLLIUS *europaeus*

GLOBE FLOWER

H 75cm/30in   S 1m/3ft 3in

The delightful globe flower is a hardy herbaceous perennial found growing in damp meadows. It produces globelike lemon-colored blooms from early to late summer that look something like very large buttercup flowers. The leaves are palmate and deeply cut. It prefers to have its roots well-drained, and the provision of a little gravel in the planting hole may be helpful. It has several garden hybrids.

T. *ledebouri*

H 1m/3ft 3in   S 1m/3ft 3in

Originally from eastern Siberia, this species has orange global buttercuplike flowers in early summer. It prefers sun.

Lysimachia punctata

Hemerocallis

Trollius europaeus

Primula pulverulenta

Primula florindae

Primula japonica

Polygonum bistorta 'Superbum'

Lysimachia nummularia

FERNS

The cool, damp conditions of the water garden offer the perfect opportunity to grow some of the loveliest ferns with their primeval forms and graceful, succulent fronds. There is a huge range of ferns that can be planted in or near water but included here are those ferns that actually enjoy having their feet in or right at the water's edge. Ferns require very little soil to root, but this soil should contain a large proportion of humus or sphagnum moss. Ferns can be grown in any shady position and there are very few gardens that do not have a spot where ferns will flourish.

MATTEUCCIA struthiopteris

OSTRICH FEATHER FERN

H 90cm/36in   S 45cm/18in

This trunk-forming, modestly sized hardy fern is ideal for small pools. It produces fine curving fronds (similar to ostrich feathers) and is best planted in groups so as to accent the lovely shape and delicacy of the fronds. It prefers woodland or rich soil in shade or half-shade.

ONOCLEA sensibilis

SENSITIVE FERN

H 60cm/24in   S 1m/3ft 3in

A native of Canada and central USA, this hardy fern will spread itself along the edge of streams and lakes. The light green leaves appear in early spring after the last frosts and, although leathery in texture, make a good contrast with primula and iris.

OSMUNDA regalis

ROYAL FERN

H 1.5m/5ft   S 1.5m/5ft

A native of North America, this hardy fern is ideal for boggy soil and can be used as a feature by a lake where its elegant shape looks wonderful reflected in the water. In autumn the leaves change color, first to orange then copper. The plant is slow growing and difficult to move successfully. For best results, choose a slightly shady spot where the roots can penetrate deep, moist soil.

PHYLLITIS scolopendrium

HART'S TONGUE FERN

H 35cm/14in   S 30cm/12in

An adaptable, hardy fern that grows in both dry and moist conditions, it is well suited to banks and rocky stream edges. Its bright green fronds will help give a natural and softening look to waterfalls, hard edges and wooden decks.

Matteuccia struthiopteris

Onoclea sensibilis

Osmunda regalis

Phyllitis scolopendrium

REEDS AND RUSHES

All reeds and rushes grow best with their roots in the water and though most require shallow water only, some will grow in water depths of up to 3m/10ft. They can make a dramatic display in small ponds, but they should be grown in submerged buckets or wire baskets to keep them under strict control as they are generally highly invasive and can take over an area very quickly. Choose a plant with a shape and growth habit that suits the design and size of your water garden.

ACORUS calamus variegatus

SWEET FLAG

H 1m/3ft 3in   S 30cm/12in

A hardy plant with attractive green-and-cream-striped leaves giving off a sweet smell when crushed, which is why it was used as a strewing rush. It should be planted in very shallow water, only a few centimeters deep. Other forms worth growing are the smaller *A. gramineus*, 25cm/10in tall, with finer leaves and plain grasslike foliage, and the very small *A.g. pusillus*, only 5-7.5cm/2-3in tall and not as hardy.

BUTOMUS umbellatus

FLOWERING RUSH

H 1m/3ft 3in   S 60cm/24in

A native of Europe and Asia, this hardy rush thrives in water up to 10cm/4in deep in a sunny position and has long, thin sword-shaped leaves ranging from purple to green. It flowers in midsummer, producing an attractive flowerhead of as many as 30 flowers on a stalk, resembling an upside-down umbrella.

JUNCUS effusus spiralis

CORKSCREW RUSH

H 4-5m/13-16ft   S 1m/3ft 3in

Most *Juncus* species are too vigorous to grow in gardens, but this one, which is not quite so prolific, is well worth grow-ing for its curious stems which grow in a distinct spiral shape like a corkscrew. A hardy plant, it will grow at the waterside in damp soil, and does not mind shade.

SCIRPUS lacustris

COMMON BULRUSH

H 2.4m/8ft   S 1m/3ft 3in

S. lacustris, everyone's idea of the classic water's edge rush, tends, however, to be too tall and prolific for the smaller water garden. Its tall green stems and fat brown pokerlike heads provide perfect cover for wildfowl. It is hardy, but likes sun. There are three interesting variegated forms: *S.l.* 'Zebrinus', with yellow horizontal bands round the stems, *S.l.* 'Pictus', which has green-white stripes and *S.l.* 'Albescens', with green and yellow-white stems.

S. tabernaemontani zebrinus

ZEBRA RUSH

H 1.2m/4ft   S 60cm/24in

Sometimes nicknamed the porcupine quill rush, this hardy rush has unusual cream and white horizontal markings on its variegated stem. Any plain green stems should be cut out or the plant may revert. This rush favors shallow water and a sunny situation.

TYPHA latifolia

REED-MACE or FALSE BULRUSH

H 2-2.4m/6ft 6in-8ft   S 1m/3ft 3in

A familiar pond-edge plant in Eurasia and North America, this plant is the false bulrush. It has gray-green spiky leaves and tall brown pokers. It is good for the edges of large lakes but *T. minima*, reaching a height of only 75cm/30in, is better suited to small gardens.

Typha latifolia

Scirpus tabernaemontani zebrinus

Acorus calamus variegatus

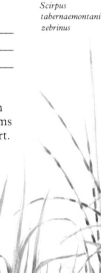

Typha minima

GRASSES AND SEDGES

There are several attractive grasses that grow well at the pond edge, and which, together with sedges, have some lovely ornamental varieties. They are useful because their roots are effective in binding the soil at the edge of streams and ponds. Don't be too eager to cut them back in winter as they can look wonderful sparkling next to the water on frosty mornings.

ARUNDO donax

GIANT REED

H 2.4-5m/8-16ft   S 3-4m/10-13ft

A fine, dramatic half-hardy plant, from southern Europe across to Iran, India, China and Japan, with tall, thick stems topped by long blue-gray leaves. It enjoys damp, sandy soils in a sunny position near the waterside, and may need protection round the base in cold winters. There is a less hardy form, *A.d. variegata,* which has leaves broadly striped with creamy-white.

CAREX stricta 'Bowles Golden'

H 30cm/12in   S 20cm/8in

With its bright yellow foliage, this sedge should be given an eye-catching position at a moist pool edge. Plant it in large groups along the edge of a stream or lake. It is an excellent foreground plant for a background of willows, or makes a good background to iris.

CYPERUS alternifolius

UMBRELLA GRASS

H 1m/3ft 3in   S 1m/3ft 3in

A native of Madagascar, this highly decorative tender sedge can be grown in a sunny position in shallow water or on the bank. It produces tall graceful stems with

TOP *Cyperus alternifolius*

RIGHT *Carex stricta* 'Bowles Golden'

Miscanthus sacchariflorus

a fine 'umbrella' of slender leaves, making a striking contrast with large broad-leaved waterside plants.

C. *longus*

SWEET GALINGALE

H 1-1.2m/3ft 3in-4ft   S 1m/3ft 3in

A native of wet meadows in southern Europe and southern central Asia, this half-hardy sedge produces tall arched slender stems of dark green with drooping clusters of red-brown flowers and seedheads. It requires sun and moisture and is a useful plant for binding the banks of large ponds. It is prolific, but growing it in a very dry situation will restrict it.

ERIOPHORUM *angustifolium*

COMMON COTTON GRASS

H 30-45cm/12-18in   S 30cm/12in

Ideal for a bog garden or shallow water approximately 13mm/½in deep, this hardy plant prefers a slightly acid soil and has narrow grasslike leaves with fluffy white cotton heads in summer. It is a native of northern Europe.

GLYCERIA *aquatica variegata*

MANNA GRASS

H 1m/3ft 3in   S indefinite

This hardy plant is worth growing for its attractive variegated green and cream, grasslike foliage and makes a good show in small ponds where it will not grow taller than 75cm/30in if planted in baskets.

MISCANTHUS *sacchariflorus*

H 2.4m/8ft   S 2m/6ft 6in

An imposing hardy grass from East Asia, *M. sacchariflorus* grows slowly to form large clumps with thick, jointed stems covered from top to bottom with long, flat fluttering dark green leaves. It looks particularly good when grown to contrast with the large leaves of *Gunnera* or *Rheum palmatum* and is tall enough to make a useful windbreak. Grow in any moist soil, in a sunny position.

M. *sinensis* 'Zebrinus'

H 2m/6ft 6in   S 2m/6ft 6in

An attractive garden addition, this handsome variegated hardy grass begins to

Spartina pectinata aureo-marginata (detail, right)

show gold stripes around midsummer and will continue to look good until the first frosts. It produces white, feathery flowerheads in autumn.

PHALARIS *arundinacea*

RIBBON GRASS

H 60cm-1m/24in-3ft 3in   S 1m/3ft 3in

Also known as 'Gardener's Garters', this attractive hardy grass is native to river banks in Europe, north central Asia, northern USA and southern Canada. It will grow in wet or dry soil in sun, but will become invasive in a rich, moist environment. The variegated 'Picta' form has green and white markings.

SPARTINA *pectinata*

PRAIRIE CORDGRASS

H 2m/6ft 6in   S 1m/3ft 3in

A hardy grass native to the prairies of midwestern USA where it grows in marshy hollows. It prefers a moist soil in sun and makes a good show in large gardens but is too invasive for smaller ones. The variety *S. aureo-marginata* features long ribbonlike leaves.

FLOATING & SUBMERGED AQUATICS

◆

WATER LILIES

Water lilies, and species related or similar to them, are happiest in still waters where they can send their strong white roots down into deep mud on the pool bottom and extend their thick rhizomes over the soil's surface. New stems always grow to the depth of the water, so a root taken from a plant in 90cm/36in of water and planted in either deeper or shallower water will produce stems to its new depth. Some species, however, are suited to deep water, others to very shallow water, as will be seen from the individual plants that follow. The stems of water lilies slow down any slight flow through a lake or pond and will accelerate silting up. Because of this, and also their vigorous growth pattern, water lilies are best planted in wire baskets for easier maintenance of the plants (see pp. 144-5). There are very many beautiful forms, including some tender species suitable only for warmer climates, but even if you have only a small water feature include just one or two of a dwarf variety such as *Nymphaea pygmaea alba*. Hardy water lilies belong to only two genera, *Nymphaea* and *Nuphar*, the latter better suited to water over 1.8m/6ft deep, and acidic waters. Both are greedy feeders and need a rich heavy loam soil.

Nymphaea 'Escarboucle'

APONOGETON distachyus

WATER HAWTHORN

D 30cm-1m/12in-3ft 3in   S several meters

Although not a water lily, this popular hardy pond plant produces long strap-like leaves of a dark green or brown color. It has white, scented, forked waxy flowers with black-purple anthers from spring to late summer. It needs a rich planting medium to produce plenty of blooms. Plant in pots or baskets. In frost-free ponds, it will flower well into winter.

NUPHAR lutea

BRANDY BOTTLE

D up to 90cm/36in   S 90cm/36in

This hardy water lily has a faint alcoholic scent, hence its common name. It can be found growing wild on European ponds and canals, and has fairly small, round yellow flowers about 7.5cm/3in across, that rise clear above its lush leaves.
The North American species, *N. advena*, has slightly larger flowers.

NYMPHAEA alba

D up to 90cm/36in   S 90cm/36in

N. alba is a hardy water lily with beautiful white fragrant flowers up to 20cm/8in across in midsummer, and almost circular leaves, rather broader than the flowers. It is a native of lakes and slow-flowing rivers across Europe. Two cultivars are *N.a.* 'Mme-Wilfron Gonnêre', a very attractive double pink water lily giving a fine display of blooms, and the similarly named *N.a.* 'Gonnêre', which is plain white.

N. × 'Ellisiana'

D 30-45cm/12-18in

A water lily with striking red flowers with dark red centers.

N. 'Escarboucle'

D up to 45cm/18in   S 1m/3ft 3in

This is an excellent water lily for the medium to large garden pool or pond. It

Nymphaea odorata 'Alba'

N. × *marliacea* 'Chromatella'

D up to 1m/3ft 3in

A robust, free-flowering lily with pale yellow blooms and brown and green mottled leaves.

N. *odorata*

D 15-30cm/6-12in

This lily, a native of North America, is popular for its scented white flowers, up to 7.5cm/3in across, with similar-sized green leaves with attractive red undersides.

N. *pygmaea alba*

D up to 30cm/12in   S 50cm/20in

A good choice for small ponds and even sinks and tubs, this lily needs only shallow water to cover its crown. It has white flowers 3.5cm/1½in across, which feature attractive bright green sepals. Another miniature cultivar worth growing for its flat, finely marked leaves and yellow flowers is *N.p.* 'Helvola'.

N. 'Sunrise'

D over 1m/3ft 3in

A water lily with rich yellow flowers up to 25cm/10in across, with unusual curved petals, hairy stems and green leaves with red-brown undersides.

grows best in shallow water and can be slow to establish. The initial flowering is slightly paler in color than subsequent years' flowers, which are a deep red.

N. 'Gladstoniana'

D up to 2m/6ft 6in

This water lily is an excellent choice for deep ponds and lakes. It has masses of very large pure white flowers, as much as 50cm/20in across, with golden stamens, in midsummer. The leaves may also be as wide as the flowers.

N. 'Laydekeri Fulgens'

D up to 1m/3ft 3in

A very striking water lily with free-blooming red flowers up to 10cm/4in in diameter and green leaves.

ABOVE *Nymphaea* 'Gladstoniana'

TOP *Nymphaea* × *marliacea* 'Chromatella'

FLOATING PLANTS

Floating plants, those that are not rooted, include some of the oxygenators (see right); some are surface-floating while others are completely or partly submerged. They spread very rapidly, and care should be taken to ensure that they can be removed easily from the water. In general, they require a water depth of between 30cm/12in and 90cm/36in.

HYDROCHARIS morsus-ranae

FROGBIT	
D up to 1m/3ft 3in	S to 2m/6ft 6in

A hardy perennial, frogbit, with its small, bronze-green kidney-shaped leaves on slender stems and tiny, three-petaled white flowers with a yellow spot in late summer, looks rather like a miniature water lily. It flourishes in sun in still, acid water. In winter it dies down after producing terminal buds, or turions, which lie on the bottom of the pond until the following spring when they begin to grow and rise to the surface.

ORONTIUM aquaticum

GOLDEN CLUB	
D 15-20cm/6-8in	S 40cm/16in

This hardy plant needs water about 30cm/12in deep and full sun to thrive. In shallow water the flower stems reach a height of up to 45cm/18in. Both leaves and flowers are attractive: pure white, gold-tipped pokers in spring and large, waxy green leaves with silver undersides, which catch the light reflected from the water. In deeper water, the leaves of *O. aquaticum* should be allowed to float on the water's surface.

STRATIOTES aloides

WATER SOLDIER	
D to 1m/3ft 3in	S 30cm/12in

This large hardy perennial is mostly submerged, its bright green, sharp-edged leaves spreading out across the surface of the water to a width of up to 30cm/12in, rather like the top of a pineapple. It will produce small white flowers in summer. It prefers limestone waters and sun, and will grow vigorously in these conditions.

TRAPA natans

WATER CHESTNUT	
D shallow water	S indefinite

The water chestnut is a hardy annual, native to Europe and naturalized in North America. It produces trailing stems with bronze and green floating leaves, looking slightly like holly, on swollen stalks. The large black spiny seeds resemble a large horse-chestnut and are delicious to eat, either raw or roasted (they are a familiar ingredient in Chinese cooking). However, they rarely ripen or set seed in temperate climates where the summers are not warm enough.

UTRICULARIA vulgaris

BLADDERWORT	
D to 1m/3ft 3in	S indefinite

This hardy carniverous plant produces feathery floating leaves with tiny bladder-like structures which catch small creatures such as daphnia. It also produces tiny, yellow snapdragonlike flowers on stems above the water's surface.

OXYGENATING PLANTS

Although these are underwater plants, some, like *Hottonia palustris*, produce flowers above the water surface.
As with the floating plants, oxygenators grow prolifically during summer and will need to be thinned out every autumn; they should not be allowed to take up more than a third of the pool's volume. Rooted plants can be planted in wire baskets to control them more easily. Propagation is by division, and plants can be introduced simply by weighting the stems and dropping them to the pool bottom. All these plants are hardy.

CALLITRICHE palustris

WATER STARWORT	
D shallow or deep water	S indefinite

The pale green foliage of water starwort is an attractive star shape, as its common name suggests. *C. palustris* makes growth in early spring, while *C. autumnalis* stays active in winter.

Orontium aquaticum

Hydrocharis morsus-ranae

Stratiotes aloides

CERATOPHYLLUM demersum

HORNWORT

D minimum 30cm/12in   S indefinite

This plant has whorls of dark green leaves round its stems. A brittle plant, segments will break off easily and root, making it an easy plant to establish. It enjoys deep pool conditions and sun.

ELODEA canadensis

CANADIAN PONDWEED

D 30-90cm/12-36in   S indefinite

A free-floating plant that grows rapidly, particularly in a new pond. It has numerous tiny, attractive dark green leaves and, as well as being an excellent oxygenator, is good for fish food and for spawning.

Utricularia vulgaris

HOTTONIA palustris

WATER VIOLET

D to 1m/3ft 3in   S 50cm/20in

Regarded as the prettiest of all oxygenators, this plant has bright green ferny leaves and pale mauve flowers that grow 10-12cm/4-5in above the water while the leaves remain submerged. The buds, which are produced late on in the year, fall to the bottom of the pool in winter to reemerge the following spring to start up new growth. It requires sun.

LEMNA minor

COMMON DUCKWEED

D shallow or deep water   S indefinite

A familiar sight in wild ponds and ditches, duckweed, another free-floating plant, is a favorite with garden fish. A hardy annual, it produces a mass of tiny green disks on long stems.

Trapa natans

L. trisulca

STAR DUCKWEED

D shallow or deep water   S indefinite

A less prolific variety, with oval, transparent green fronds with thin strands; it is an excellent purifier.

MYRIOPHYLLUM spicatum

MILFOIL

D 1m/3ft 3in   S indefinite

A rooted perennial plant with attractive red, branched stems and olive-colored leaves, it resembles hornwort except that its structure is flatter. In summer it produces tiny red and yellow flowers and is an excellent purifier.

POTAMOGETON crispus

CURLED PONDWEED

D shallow to 50cm/20in   S 1m/3ft 3in

With its wavy-edged bronze-hued leaves, 7.5cm/3in long and 13mm/½in wide, this submerged weed resembles seaweed. The leaves will only change to a red color in strong light.

RANUNCULUS aquatilis

WATER CROWFOOT

D up to 1m/3ft 3in   S indefinite

A shallow-rooting plant, mostly afloat, and characterized by a mass of white buttercup-shaped flowers on a carpet of green leaves on or just above the water surface in spring. The plant has two types of leaves: those under the water surface are fronded and threadlike while the floating leaves are flat and segmented with three lobes. For it to become an oxygenator, it requires deeper water (up to 1m/3ft 3in) otherwise the underwater leaves may not develop.

Ranunculus aquatilis

SHRUBS & TREES

◇

SHRUBS

Apart from *Cornus* and *Spiraea*, very few shrubs will tolerate having their roots in water, but there are a number that grow happily at the water's edge.

Three bamboo species have been included in this section although bamboo is a giant grass rather than a true shrub; their size and the fact that most are evergreen suit them well to this category. Bamboos are prolific growers but can be restricted by periodically cutting off some of the lateral rhizomes at the edge of the clump that spread horizontally before throwing up new canes.

Although not essentially a shrub, *Phormium* is included here since it is grown with this category. It provides a sharp architectural feature.

ARUNDINARIA *japonica*

H 4-5m/13-16ft	S 3-4m/10-13ft

A large, handsome, dark green glossy-leaved bamboo from central and southern Japan, which makes dense thickets of canes with ribbon-shaped dark green glossy leaves. It is hardy and thrives in moist soil in half-shade. However, it is a vigorous grower and is better suited to large gardens.

AZALEA

H 1.2-2.4m/4-8ft	S 2m/6ft 6in

Azaleas are the same plant type as *Rhododendron*, but they are nearly always thought of as separate groups. Azaleas, which have a limited northerly range, are nearly all deciduous except for the ever-green Japanese varieties. They are of medium height, which makes them ideal for most garden settings. All azaleas prefer a moist humus-rich acid soil and dappled or half-shade; provided there is no trace of lime in the soil they make good waterside shrubs. There is a wide choice of varieties, from the Ghent azaleas which are very hardy with fragrant flowers, to the Rustica hybrids which grow to 1.8m/6ft high and as much across and produce mainly pink double flowers in early summer. For smaller gardens, plant the Kurume azaleas, which never grow more than approximately 76cm/2ft 6in tall. These azaleas have mainly pink or red flowers in spring.

CORNUS *alba* 'Sibirica'

SIBERIAN DOGWOOD	
H 1.5-2.4m/5-8ft	S 2-2.4m/6ft 6in-8ft

The dogwoods are attractive hardy deciduous shrubs, generally grown for their fine foliage and brightly colored bark in winter. They are particularly suitable for planting by ponds and streams and like a rich woodland soil. All types will thrive in sun or light shade. *C.a.* 'Sibirica' is one of the most striking of its type, with its red, shiny stems in winter. It should be cut back every 2 or 3 years to encourage the growth of new colored stems.

C. *controversa*

TABLE DOGWOOD	
H 14m/46ft	S 3m/10ft

Although mainly grown for its spectacular red leaf color in autumn, it flowers in midsummer giving broad white clusters 7.5cm/3in wide. The variegated form has leaves bordered with white. It prefers moist rich soils and is extremely suitable for growing in a pot next to a small pond where its growth can be kept under control.

C. *florida*

FLOWERING DOGWOOD	
H 4m/13ft	S very varied

Native to the USA, this dogwood will grow in very wet soils. It has very attractive white bracts.

C. *kousa*

H 3m/10ft	S 2.4-3m/8-10ft

This dogwood has rounded white flower bracts in midsummer which are followed by strawberrylike edible fruits ripening in late summer.

C. *nuttallii*

MOUNTAIN DOGWOOD	
H 10m/32ft	S very varied

A free-flowering dogwood that is less hardy than the others mentioned. It has very large white-cream bracts in midsummer, and likes sun or semishade.

C. *stolonifera*

AMERICAN DOGWOOD	
H 2m/6ft 6in	S very varied

Like *C. alba* 'Sibirica', this dogwood has dark purplish-red shoots. It is another species that needs cutting back every 2 to 3 years to produce its colored stems.

HYDRANGEA

H and S according to species

This large family of plants is happy growing in or near the water. They prefer a humus-rich, acid soil. There are many varieties both in color and form. Most species of *Hydrangea* are hardy, but they will also tolerate more tropical conditions.

KALMIA latifolia

CALICO BUSH

H 1.8-3m/6-10ft   S 1.5m/5ft

K. latifolia produces clusters of umbrella-like pink flowers in summer. Like rhododendrons, which belong to the same family, *Kalmias* are hardy evergreens and are committed lime-haters and will not grow in alkaline soil. They require a moist, well-drained acid/peat soil and a cool, lightly shaded position.

PHORMIUM cookianum

MOUNTAIN FLAX

H 1m/3ft 3in   S 1.2-1.5m/4-5ft

Native to damp mountain scrub and grassland of New Zealand, this half-hardy spreading plant is ideal for smaller water gardens as a background for other lower water plants. It has widespread stems with rather dingy green and orange tubular flowers. The seedheads are very decorative. It needs protection from cold winds and should be screened from north-east winds and from frosts. It will grow in different soil types and tolerates half-shade but is happiest when close to water in enriched soil in full sun.

P. tenax

NEW ZEALAND FLAX

H 1.5-2.4m/5-8ft   S 2m/6ft 6in

Although rather stiff in habit, this plant's curious flower spikes, carrying clusters of dull red flowers that become black bunches of short banana-shaped seedpods, make it a most unusual feature in a large water garden. Like *P. cookianum*, *P. tenax* is half-hardy and requires protection; its two cultivars, 'Purpureum' and 'Variegatum' are slightly less hardy than the parent.

PHYLLOSTACHYS aureosulcata

YELLOW-GROOVE BAMBOO

H 4-5m/13-16ft   S to 5m/16ft

A bamboo from Japan and China that is used extensively in Japanese gardens to emphasize or contrast with stone groupings near water or dry streams, or as a feature plant in a small patio area. It takes its name from the fine yellow stripe that runs up the stem. It tolerates a drier soil than the *Arundinaria* bamboos, but in rich, moist conditions, *P. aureosulcata* will grow very rapidly.

Phyllostachys aureosulcata

Phyllostachys nigra

Sasa palmata

Sasa veitchii

Azalea sp. and *Rhododendron* sp.

large-leaved treelike types are more suited to sheltered, warmer positions while the small-leaved shrubby and dwarf varieties will thrive in more exposed areas. With such a vast selection of leaf shapes and colors, with flowers ranging from red, white and pink to purple and yellow, choice must be simply one of personal preference.

SASA palmata

H to 2m/6ft 6in   S indefinite

A hardy large-leaved bamboo which is invasive but does well even in cold areas. Its large leaves make a good feature by water. It grows rapidly when given plenty of moisture and is also a good bamboo to put in a pot as a specimen.

S. veitchii

KUMA BAMBOO GRASS

H 60-90cm/24-36in   S indefinite

A good-looking bamboo from southern Japan, *S. veitchii* is very invasive but worth growing for its mass of purple-green canes and bright green leaves all summer. In autumn the leaves, which remain all winter, develop white markings.

SORBARIA aitchisonii

FALSE SPIRAEA

H 2.4-3m/8-10ft   S 3-4m/10-13ft

This hardy deciduous shrub has elegant feathery leaves on red stems and an attractive bushy habit. It produces creamy white plumes of flowers in late summer. It prefers a moist peaty soil in full sun or light shade.

P. nigra

BLACK BAMBOO

H 4-5m/13-16ft   S to 5m/16ft

This bamboo forms a large clump of graceful, arching stems. The canes are green the first year and turn black to provide a useful and striking contrast to other plants. This is a hardy plant and it prefers half-shade in any type of soil.

RHODODENDRON

H and S according to species

Ranging in size from small shrubs to large trees, rhododendrons, which have a wide spread across the world, are mainly evergreen and, provided the soil is acid, will grow happily in well-drained soil at the poolside. There is a wide variety to suit any sized garden. The

TREES

Important considerations whether designing a water garden near existing trees or when planning new trees for a water feature are shade and leaf drop: too much of either will mean dark smelly water, whereas no shade at all will result in too high water temperatures and fast evaporation. Therefore, choose trees with a light leaf canopy as well as interesting leaf shape and coloring. The delightful acers are particularly good for the waterside as are species such as *Salix* and *Taxodium,* which actually like getting their feet wet. Other trees, however, should be planted on raised banks or in higher, well-drained soil near to the water's edge.

ACER griseum

PAPERBARK MAPLE

H 14m/46ft	S 1-2m/3ft 3in-6ft 6in

A native of China, this tree is usually suited to larger water features. It has ornamental peeling orange bark and red-orange leaves in autumn. It prefers half shade and a good deep woodland soil, and can tolerate drier conditions.

A. japonicum

JAPANESE or FULL-MOON MAPLE

H 3-6m/10-20ft	S 3-6m/10-20ft

The Japanese maples, *A. japonicum* and *A. palmatum* (see above right), have red and gold leaves in autumn, and both have many cultivars. *A.j.* 'Aureum' forms a rounded bush, about 3m/10ft by 3m/10ft, which retains its beautiful yellow color while in leaf, but is very slow-growing. *A.j.* 'Aconitifolium' is again slow-growing, but the short-lived autumn color, bright orange turning scarlet, is spectacular. This tree reaches about 3m/10ft tall with a spread of about 5m/16ft. The foliage, which is finely divided in twos, is one of the most delicate of any tree available.

A. negundo

ASH-LEAVED MAPLE or BOX ELDER

H 14m/46ft	S 1-2m/3ft 3in-6ft 6in

With its cultivar, *A.n.* 'Variegatum', the ash-leaved maple is native to the swamps and stream sides of central and east North America. In spring it produces yellow-green tassels of flowers and yellow foliage in autumn. *A.n.* 'Variegatum' is useful for bringing light and color into a small space and will help reflect light on to the water surface.

A. palmatum

H to 6m/20ft	S 6m/20ft

This, the most striking of the Japanese maples, looks wonderful next to water where its lovely green foliage can be reflected. If possible, plant this tree in groups of three. *A. palmatum* has a dwarf cultivar, *A.p.* 'Dissectum', which, if allowed to grow, will eventually make a round-headed tree about 2m/6ft 6in high with a 3m/10ft spread. With its soft, delicate foliage it makes an ideal tree for a small garden and can be planted in a pot next to a pool or water sculpture.

ALNUS glutinosa

COMMON or BLACK ALDER

H 19m/62ft	S 3m/10ft

The alders, hardy deciduous trees, are generally fast-growing. They thrive in moist soil and sometimes even in the water, and are slow to come into leaf in spring. They produce early catkins which make a wonderful show when little else is flowering. *A. glutinosa*, native to Europe, west Asia and North Africa, grows wild in boggy land and on riversides. It has rough bark and small dark leaves, which are retained till late autumn. Slightly invasive, it is best kept under control and is not recommended for a small water garden.

Acer palmatum 'Dissectum'

Metasequoia glyptostroboides (left) and *Betula pendula* 'Youngii' (right)

Taxodium distichum

A. incana 'Laciniata'

CUT-LEAVED ALDER

H 10m/32ft S 3m/10ft

This cut-leafed alder is a highly ornamental tree and has a tall trunk and
delicate lacy gray leaves. It prefers a damp
soil and would be a good tree for a bog
garden.

BETULA occidentalis

WATER BIRCH

H 6-7.5m/20-25ft S 3m/10ft

Native to north-west America where it
grows thickly along the sides of streams,
this birch produces dark green leaves and
shiny, very dark brown bark. Like all
birches, it is deciduous and hardy.

B. papyrifera

CANOE or PAPERBARK BIRCH

H 6m/20ft S 2m/6ft 6in

This is an ideal birch for the bog garden,
a native of North America and Canada.
A tall thin upright open-headed tree, it
allows light through its foliage but has
fairly large irregular tooth-shaped leaves
that turn yellow in autumn. Its smooth
white bark peels in paperlike layers. If
possible, plant several specimens of this
tree close to the water where the reflections of the white bark can be admired.

B. pendula

H 18m/60ft S 3m/10ft

Native to Europe and Asia Minor, this
birch produces the familiar lamb's tail
catkins in spring and is a popular garden
tree in Europe and North America for its

graceful weeping branches and silver-white bark. It grows easily on any soil and in any situation, sun or shade. *B.p.* 'Youngii' is slower growing with a more accentuated weeping habit, reaching a height of 4-5m/13-16ft, with a spread of the same. *B.p.* 'Dalecarlica', the Swedish birch, has beautiful pendulous branchlets and feathery leaves. It can be pruned to keep its height at around 7-8m/23-26ft, and spread about 2m/6ft 6in.

CORYLUS maxima 'Purpurea'

PURPLE-LEAVED HAZELNUT

H 3m/10ft   S 3m/10ft

This hardy hazel has rich purple young leaves in summer that change to red in autumn. It enjoys damp soil and sun or shade, and produces catkins in mid-winter. The green-brown fringed fruits in autumn are, like those of the common hazel, *C. avellana,* good to eat.

KOWHAI sophora tetraptera

H 6m/20ft   S 2m/6ft 6in

This most beautiful half-hardy flowering tree from New Zealand is not strictly a water-loving tree but will tolerate being planted next to water. The beautiful pendulous yellow flowers come in early spring when most of the leaves fall. In sheltered conditions, this plant can be grown in Europe.

LIRIODENDRON tulipifera

TULIP TREE, WHITEWOOD

H 15-18m/50-60ft   S 3-4m/10-13ft

One of the most handsome hardy deciduous shade trees, this tree blooms with delicate tuliplike yellow-green flowers with prominent stamens in early summer. Its midgreen leaves are fiddle-shaped and lustrous, turning gold in autumn. The tree needs full sunlight and rich, moist soil and thrives when planted next to water – if it has insufficient moisture, the leaves tend to turn brown. Since it

has a very deep root system, do not plant it next to a concrete pool. In the right conditions it will grow at least 1.5m/5ft annually.
A slightly smaller variety, *L.t.* 'Aureo-marginatum', has identical flowers but its leaves are heavily margined in yellow. For a small garden, this tree can be trained and kept under control by regular pruning as necessary.

METASEQUOIA glyptostroboides

DAWN REDWOOD

H 16m/52ft   S 6m/20ft

This impressive hardy deciduous tree is native to China and is the last remaining member of a very old genus, thought until 1944 to be extinct and existing only in fossil form. It has dark gray, peeling bark and bright green foliage changing to pink and gold in autumn. The cones are cylindrical and pendulous. The tree enjoys moist soil and a sunny or partially shaded position; in these conditions it grows about 1.2m/4ft annually. Along with the swamp cypress, it is one of the few deciduous conifers.

POPULUS alba

WHITE POPLAR, ABELE

H 30m/100ft   S 3-4m/10-13ft

The poplars are hardy deciduous trees and *P. alba* has handsome smooth white or gray bark with diamond-shaped markings. It is unusual in that it will survive saltwater spray in coastal settings and will grow well on sandy soil.

SALIX alba 'Britzensis'

H 2m/6ft 6in   S 1m/3ft 3in

This fast-growing willow can be restricted to a low habit if pruned hard every year. Hard pruning will also maintain a good stem color on new growth and should produce bright red shoots every winter. A hardy tree, it has a limited northerly range and likes sun and very wet soil.

S. × chrysocoma

GOLDEN WEEPING WILLOW

H 20m/65ft   S 3-4m/10-13ft

The hardy deciduous weeping willows with their drooping graceful branches of narrow leaves have long been familiar waterside trees. The lovely golden color of this particular willow has made it increasingly more popular. It does, however, require full sun.

S. fragilis

CRACK WILLOW

H 25m/82ft   S 4-5m/13-16ft

Native to riverbanks of Europe and west Siberia south to Iran, this willow has narrow, toothed green leaves and twigs that snap off easily, giving the tree its name. These will root and form new plants.

S. matsudana 'Tortuosa'

CORKSCREW WILLOW

H 10m/32ft   S 2m/6ft 6in

Looking rather like an outsize bonsai tree, this willow with its twisted twigs and contorted branches looks best when leafless. It has hairy silver catkins in early spring. It does well in any damp or wet soil and prefers full sun. In the right conditions it is fast-growing.

TAXODIUM distichum

SWAMP or BALD CYPRESS

H 30m/100ft   S 3m/10ft

This hardy deciduous conifer comes from the swamps of south-eastern USA and has small moss-green frondlike leaves that turn rich brown in autumn with tassels of yellow flowers. Slow-growing, it prefers to be near water where its roots will show above the waterline, and in a sunny position.

TENDER PLANTS

The following plants are examples of some of the more spectacular tender species that are popular in tropical or subtropical water gardens. Some of the smaller examples can also be grown successfully in indoor pools and in water gardens in temperate regions.

ADIANTUM aethiopicum

MAIDENHAIR FERN

H 60cm/24in   S 1m/3ft 3in

This tender fern, native to Australia and New Zealand, is much valued for its soft foliage. Young foliage is often a light yellow-green color. It needs moisture and peaty soil with some sand, and looks superb in a pot.

CALLISTEMON viminalis

WEEPING BOTTLEBRUSH

H 6m/20ft   S 2m/6ft 6in

This colorful shrub is tender and really only suitable for subtropical gardens. It has rosy-lilac brushlike flower spikes in spring and pendulous light green foliage. It prefers plenty of moisture but will tolerate some dry conditions; it grows best in wet soils next to water. It makes an excellent plant by a small water feature, and can be grown indoors in more northerly climates.

CYPERUS papyrus

NILE GRASS, PAPYRUS

H 2.4m/8ft   S 3-4m/10-13ft

This, the 'reed' from which the Egyptians made the first paper, is a subtropical tender sedge that can be grown in a pot by an indoor water feature, or, in warmer areas, used as a foliage contrast near the waterside. It is often used as an accent plant in pebble gardens.

DACRYDIUM bidwillii

BOG PINE

H 1.5m/5ft   S 1-2m/3ft 3in-6ft 6in

A small tender shrub that has attractive cypresslike foliage and, as its name suggests, an ability to grow in wet soils. The soil, however, must be rich and deep. It is an ideal bog garden plant, though only suitable for warmer climates. It prefers half-shade.

DICKSONIA antarctica

SOFT TREE FERN

H 6m/20ft   S canopy 2-3m/6ft 6in-10ft

This handsome half-hardy tree fern has a brown trunk topped by a graceful winged head of bright green fronds, 1.8m/6ft or more long, with finely divided lacy foliage. An Australian native, this fern is suitable for growing in large containers and will grow happily near water, but is only suitable for mild, frost-free climates. Old fronds must be cut away annually. The fern can be grown by an indoor water garden.

EICHHORNIA speciosa

WATER HYACINTH

H (above water) 20cm/8in   S indefinite

This beautiful tender plant thrives in tropical and subtropical climates; in Florida it became so prolific that it was a menace to boats on the St John's river and cannot now legally be transported across State lines. It has shiny round green leaves on swollen stems that allow the plant to float, and the flowers are fabulous – spikes of mauve-blue with a touch of yellow. In the northern hemisphere, the plant may be floated in an inside tank with a layer of soil and slightly warmed water.

ERYTHRINA indica

INDIAN CORAL TREE

H 8m/26ft   S 3-4m/10-13ft

A handsome flowering tender tree for large gardens, considered unsuitable for small or suburban gardens because it drops its flowers and foliage and has an invasive root system. The giant peapod-shaped flowers are bright red in winter, followed by long seed pods. The prickly bark is gray-brown and the large-leaved foliage is pale green. It can be grown only in subtropical or tropical regions and is equally at home in coastal gardens with wet, saline soils or in hot dry inland gardens.

PISTIA stratiotes

WATER LETTUCE

D shallow water   S indefinite

A short-lived tender perennial, water lettuce is a good foliage plant for the water surface and looks something like a squashed lettuce with its large, flat, pale green leaves growing out from a central point. Grown outside only in tropical and subtropical regions, it does particularly well at water temperatures above 20°C/68°F. The water lettuce is banned in Texas.

VICTORIA amazonica

VICTORIA LILY

D 2m/6ft 6in or more   S 3m/10ft

A spectacular, giant, tender water lily that needs a large pool (or deep pit containing enriched soil dug into a smaller pool) as it is a hungry feeder. The leaves can reach up to 2m/6ft 6in in diameter, and the beautiful creamy-white to pink flowers (depending on the time of day), up to 20cm/8in in diameter, have a pineapplelike scent. This lily can only be grown out of doors in equatorial regions, but is grown inside in the northern hemisphere where conditions of space and heat permit.

WATER GARDEN TECHNIQUES

Practical information on all aspects of installation and construction; pools and ponds, fountains, waterfalls, streams and watercourses – tools, leveling techniques and materials; making a bog garden; different types of bridge and laying surrounding surfaces; working with lumber; installing lighting in the water garden; planting and caring for water garden plants and trees, encouraging wildlife; care and maintenance; safety points

THERE IS no doubt that, if executed well, a water feature makes a valuable and most enjoyable asset to any garden or patio. It can, however, be time consuming and exacting to install and it may be tempting to take short cuts in order to achieve some of the lovely effects shown on the previous pages. The only good advice is – don't do it!

If you disregard the guidelines recommended in this and other chapters, use inferior materials or poor workmanship, you are asking for disaster. There can be no half-way measures when constructing a water feature: either it is done properly or it is not worth doing at all. Build a pool too near deciduous trees or shrubs, for example, and you will land yourself with a lot of work clearing black, slimy, leaf-filled water; construct a stream or fountain badly and it simply will not work properly. The best thing to do if you are at all uncertain about the cost or practicalities of a particular project is to seek the advice of a professional landscape architect or to scale down your plans to something you know you can handle.

It is essential to plan your water feature well in advance. Draw up your proposals to scale on graph paper first or superimpose cut-out shapes of the proposed feature on a black and white photograph of your garden and then ask yourself whether it fits the general design and layout of your site (see pp. 54-5). Remember to allow for the cost of the surrounding surfaces – paving, lawn and relandscaping – and the hire of special machinery and any features such as waterfalls, fountains and sculptures you may wish to install. Assess your own capabilities for tackling excavation and building work and the likelihood of having to hire experts to handle plumbing and electrical jobs. It is also important to think about the upheaval of excavation work and how you plan to dispose of large amounts of soil and rubble produced during the work.

– SUITABILITY –

There are very few locations where a pool or pond is impossible to install and most problems can be overcome provided they are planned for at the outset. You should check, for example, that there are no underlying obstructions such as old foundations, drains or power cables that will need moving or covering with special protective conduits; areas with a high water table will also not be suitable for large pools unless they can be raised above ground level.

Poor access is a factor many potential pool and pond builders fail to take into consideration. For a large pool, you will need some way of getting heavy machinery in and out of the garden as well as soil, rubble and other materials. It may be possible to remove walls and fences temporarily or even hire a crane to lift heavy items over any obstruction, but bear in mind that this will add considerably to the cost of the project.

Cost, of course, is one of the most limiting factors. If you really cannot afford to build a full-scale pool or large pond, why not consider a simpler but equally effective moving water feature, such as the water spout on p. 19 or a bog garden tub on the patio.

– TECHNIQUES –

Pool building techniques are fairly basic unless you are installing complicated shapes, and patience and careful workmanship are needed more than any special skills. Providing you can tackle

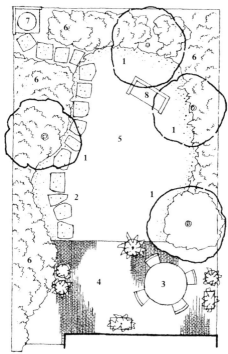

Adapting an existing garden
Redesigning your garden to include an interesting pond or pool needn't mean tremendous expense, nor even a particularly large site. This typical suburban garden plot (above) once featured the familiar formula of paved patio, central lawn and shrubby borders. A new informal water feature to break up the center of the plot (opposite) soon transformed the vista from various points around the garden, with a raised wooden deck to disguise part of the old patio and to create a change of level.

1 Trees 2 Path 3 Dining and seating area 4 Brick patio
5 Lawn 6 Shrub and flower borders 7 Compost pile
8 Bench 9 Raised wooden deck 10 Wooden bridge
11 Informal pond 12 Water lilies 13 Fountain 14 Pump
15 Lights 16 Pebble beaches 17 Bamboo screen
18 Reduced lawn area 19 Trellis above fences

simple concreting, paving and carpentry jobs, you should have no problems constructing a pond or pool and its surrounds (see pp. 126-31). Excavation methods depend on the size of hole you are making and will range from a spade and a strong back to large commercial machinery and the hire of a professional driver to operate it. But the technique remains the same – digging out, making sure you can maintain the correct water level with top-up and drainage facilities and waterproofing the sides and floor.

How you waterproof your pool will also depend on its size and shape. Premolded fiberglass pools are cheap and easy to install but tend to be small and not always easy to landscape successfully into the garden. Specially manufactured liners are more flexible for small pools and ponds and these can be professionally seamed for larger features. Some swimming pools are also sold in kit form and include a ready made pool liner.

Provided it is properly mixed and handled, concrete has excellent water-retaining properties and, with the addition of frostproofing chemicals, is ideally suited to most types of location. It is particularly good for raised and formal pools but not really good for large, naturalistic ponds. The larger and less formal a feature, the more unlikely it is you can use any type of liner and, instead, you must rely on a method known as clay puddling to make the sides and floor waterproof. Clay puddling involves molding natural clay with your hands, waterproof boots or, for really large sites, a digging machine to make a relatively effective seal. Where the natural subsoil is too porous, a commercially available clay such as Volclay can be introduced (see p. 131).

– LANDSCAPING –

Once your pool or pond is in situ, you will want to make it look like an integral part of the garden by disguising its construction and landscaping the surrounding area. The methods employed will depend very much on the size and style of your garden and the type of pool or pond banks. Surrounding surfaces will need careful thought (see pp. 70-5). Pumps, hoses and electric cables, where applicable, will also have to be disguised with careful planting or boulders. These are also perfect for hiding a constructed water's edge but take care that stones and boulders are not likely to tear a rubber or plastic liner – especially if you intend to introduce boulders into the water itself to provide a visual link between bank and pool. It makes sense to use soil excavated during construction to add a change of level to the garden. Avoid placing it in large piles where it will probably look completely unnatural.

Planting a pool and its surrounds benefits from preplanning. Aim for a good balance of shape, size and color. Large-leaved plants and tall grasses look splendid by the water's edge where they will be reflected in the surface. Offset these with smaller, low-growing varieties and lilies that grow on the water's surface, and choose some of the beautiful flowering species to add color (see pp. 94-122).

Providing access to your finished water feature by means of a path, bridge or stepping stones (see pp. 64-9 and 136-7) from other parts of the garden not only makes sense from a practical point of view, but will also emphasize the feature as something special and lead the eye to it. Moving water, too, will add interest and has the extra benefit of preventing the water stagnating.

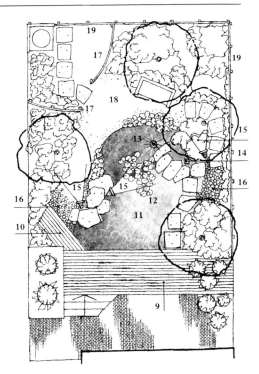

A change of level
Use soil excavated when making a pool to landscape the surrounding area. Around a formal pool, raised planting beds are more appropriate than irregular mounds, and the retaining walls are useful for keeping plant matter and soil out of the water. Face the walls with bricks or paving to match the style of the pool and its setting.

POOLS & PONDS

◆

The shape of your pool or pond should reflect the general character of its surroundings – the style of your house, garden and any neighboring property. Other chapters have dealt with the wide range of water features you can create, from large, naturalistic ponds to small, formal patio features, and how these can be successfully integrated into your own garden. A general piece of advice worthy of restating is that you should consider the suitability of any feature you are thinking of installing and look for ways it can be fitted into the natural contours of the garden – tucked into the angle of a corner, for example, or paralleling the straight edges of a formal paved area.

– ASSESSING YOUR SITE –
Formal pools will have to be mapped out on the ground using a square and a straightedge in order to reproduce the shapes as accurately as possible. Circular or oval-shaped features can be mapped out using a center peg and string, while more irregular shapes can be created by laying a length of hose, or a series of pegs and strings, along the ground until you are happy with the effect. Remember to view your proposed shape from all angles of the garden, as well as from the house – particularly from upper-storey windows, if possible – to check that it looks satisfactory no matter what angle it is seen from.

If you are lucky enough to have a big

garden, it certainly pays to make the most of it with a spectacular pond. But there is no reason why you should not install a large pool in a small garden, provided it blends well with the overall style of the setting.

Whatever size feature you settle on, you must appreciate its limitations: a small, shallow pond or pool can support only a restricted selection of plants and fish and will require extra care in winter (see pp. 148-51); a lake or large pond needs a suitable setting and will be expensive to construct.

When assessing your own site, look for natural contours that can be utilized and incorporated into your pond or pool – a low spot that is naturally damp for a pool, for example, or a ditch, natural stream bed or spring that can be used to feed or provide run-off facilities for your water feature. By using an indentation or damp hollow you will save yourself some excavation costs and have the confidence that the feature will look correctly placed in the garden.

If your site allows, the best place for a water feature such as a pond or pool is as close to the house as possible. Depending on the style of your house, you can then use linking material, such as brick, paving or a wooden-decked jetty (which acts as both a veranda and viewpoint over the water), in order to bring house and feature together. Not only do most buildings look magnificent when reflected in water, either day or night, but your pond will also be more accessible in all types of weather. If, however, you have children in the family, you may need to position a pond or pool in part of the garden where it can be safely fenced off (see pp. 152-3).

Other factors that may influence your

Types of pool

ORNAMENTAL POOL
Small pools about 3sq m/ 32sq ft can be excavated by hand or by using light machinery and then lined with butyl or concrete.

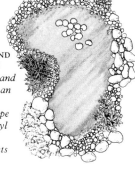

SMALL INFORMAL POND
A small natural pond can be excavated by hand or light machinery to an irregular shape about 8m/26ft long. This type of pond is usually butyl lined and the edges naturalized with plants and boulders to help them blend.

LARGE INFORMAL POND
A large pond, say, 13m/ 43ft in length, would be impracticable to line in concrete or butyl. It would have to be mechanically excavated and clay puddled.

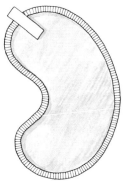

SWIMMING POOL
An in-ground swimming pool requires large excavation machinery and facilities for the removal and disposal of soil. Proximity to services for maintenance equipment may determine site. A typical 12m/39ft pool can be concrete or butyl lined.

choice of position are whether you want to install features such as a waterfall or fountain, or lights which will necessitate laying power cables from the main supply and then disguising any pumps and burying the cable at a safe depth to avoid accidental damage.

– TOOLS AND EQUIPMENT –

The size of your proposed pool or pond will influence your choice of excavation method, but only the very smallest pool can really be tackled with a pick and shovel. Professional and specialist equipment can be expensive but is easy to hire and well worth the cost in terms of the time and effort it will save you.

In order to get the most from this equipment, make sure the site is ready for the day you hire and consider hiring over a weekend when rates tend to be lower. For large pieces of machinery, make sure you have adequate access to the site and room to maneuver during operation.

As a checklist, write down on a piece of paper each stage of the job you are contemplating and the equipment you will need for each one, and assemble the appropriate tools before you start working. You will probably find that you have many of the basic tools already, but check the list on p. 128 to make sure you are not left stranded at a crucial point in the construction process.

Mechanical excavation

A mechanical excavator will make short work of one of the most tedious aspects of creating a pool or pond – that of digging the hole. There are various machines available depending on the size of hole required. A small dump-mounted backhoe is easy to operate yourself and can be hired on a daily or weekly basis. It is mainly used for digging trenches for straight-sided watercourses and is ideal for digging to a maximum depth of 1.5m/5ft in light soil. For slightly more ambitious projects, there are four-wheel drive hydraulic backhoes with front-end loaders, which are excellent machines. They will cope with most small and medium-sized pools and have the added advantage that they can be used to transport excavated soil to another part of the garden. For sloping sites, a larger bulldozer is recommended. Such a large machine is always rented with an operator. It is, however, extremely maneuverable and will produce very quick results. It is particularly useful for moving heavy soil. Very large bulldozers, or 'caterpillars', also require the services of a qualified operator and are available for rent by the hour. Being enormous, they can be employed only where there is good access, but they are capable of almost any type of excavation work in most conditions thanks to their tanklike tracks, which give them excellent traction over sloping and difficult ground. These 'caterpillars' excavate so quickly and efficiently that they are almost always used in conjunction with dump trucks to remove the soil. Although this adds to the cost, it is the only way to make proper use of such an excavator.

A local plant rental company should be able to advise you on the suitability of a particular machine, but it is worth bearing in mind that a fast, efficient, heavy-duty machine, operated by a professional well acquainted with the controls, could well work out less expensive on an hourly basis than a less powerful digger that takes you all weekend or longer to learn to use properly.

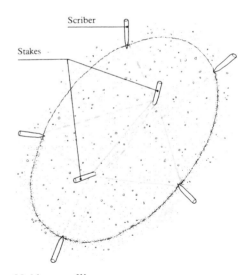

Making a right-angle
In order to maintain an accurate right-angle when constructing a formal pool, it is a good idea to make a large-scale square using lengths of wood. Lengths cut to the ratio 3:4:5 will guarantee an accurate 90° angle. Always double check measurements at every stage.

Making an ellipse
An ellipse shape for a pool or pond can be drawn using stakes and a loop of string. Place the loop over two fixed stakes and, using a scriber to keep the string taut, mark out an elliptical shape on the ground. The position of the stakes will determine the shape of the ellipse – the closer together the stakes are, the more circular the shape.

Hand tools

The excavation of small garden pools and ponds requires only ordinary tools, and many of these you may already have. Top of the list for any type of construction work should be a large level and a 3m/10ft straightedge – usually a piece of planed, warp-free wood or length of metal will do – to ensure that surfaces are straight and level. For the same purpose, you will need a wooden post approximately 1.2m × 5 × 5cm/4ft × 2 × 2in to act as a level reference in the middle of the pool, and a series of wooden pegs 30 × 2.5 × 2.5cm/12 × 1 × 1in to mark out the shape and keep it level.

Other essential tools include a good wood saw, a heavy mallet to knock the post and pegs into the ground and a tape measure for checking and double checking all calculations. For a small hole, a spade or garden fork and shovel will be adequate, although a pick will be invaluable for breaking any hard, clay-type soils. You will inevitably need some means of transporting excavated soil in the form of a sturdy wheelbarrow. Try to get one with a large, inflatable tire, which makes moving heavy loads much easier.

Tools for concreting

If you intend to line your pool or watercourse with concrete, you will need a shovel, wheelbarrow and pliers. You use the pliers to twist reinforcing chicken wire into the appropriate shape for your excavation. If you are mixing up your own concrete, then a bucket makes a convenient measuring device for the different ingredients. After pouring the concrete, use a trowel or float to smooth it over. Also handy is a piece of rigid board for mixing the concrete on.

– LEVELING AND EXCAVATING –

First, mark out your chosen shape on the lawn or soil using a length of string wrapped round pegs, or a garden hose. Check this shape from all angles and, when satisfied, strip the turf from the area to be excavated by cutting it into long strips with a sharp-edged spade before lifting. Roll the turfs, root side out, like a jelly roll, keep them damp and store them carefully for repairs elsewhere in the garden or to edge your pool, pond or watercourse when completed.

You can now start to remove the topsoil, which should be kept carefully on one side for use when planting or returfing. Never mix it with subsoil, rocks or rubble or contaminate it with cement powder. Next, excavate the subsoil, using it to form mounds or landscaped contours around the site area, or have it hauled away if you will not be needing it later. Remove subsoil to approximately the correct depth – a minimum of 60cm/24in and a maximum of about 1.2m/4ft. If possible, angle the sides of the pool or pond at about 20°. This will make concreting easier and also allow any ice to rise in winter instead of it expanding and cracking the sides. Also, try to incorporate a shelf running right round a pond or pool excavation to accommodate baskets of waterside plants near the surface. The shelf should be about 25cm/10in below the final water level and 30cm/12in wide. A trench for a watercourse should be straight sided.

It is vitally important to ensure that the sides of the excavation are level – water always finds a perfect level and it will reveal instantly the slightest discrepancy. To achieve a level excavation, place the 1.2m/4ft post already mentioned in the center of the site and drive

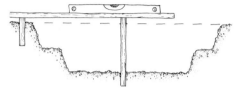

Leveling a pool
A length of planed, warp-free wood long enough to run from a stake in the center of the pool to a peg on the bank will act as a straightedge, allowing a level to be placed along the top edge for an accurate reading. Make a reading at every stage of construction.

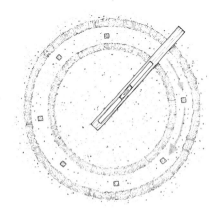

Leveling a circular pool
You can check that a circular water feature is level by pivoting the straightedge to different points around the perimeter banks. A narrow shelf approximately 25cm/10in below the final level of the bank is useful for positioning baskets of waterside plants.

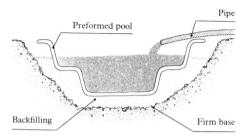

Installing a preformed pool
Excavate a hole to roughly the right size and shape and insert the mold on a firm base of rubble and sand. Gradually filling the pool with water as you backfill the hole will maintain stability, but check repeatedly with a straightedge and level.

it into the ground. If you rest the straightedge between this point and one of the smaller 30cm/12in side pegs hammered into the bank, a level along the top edge will tell you where any adjustment needs to be made. Repeat this right round the pool area or length of channel using a series of side pegs to ensure a completely level finish.

When you are certain the levels are accurate, remove any sharp stones or metal objects, which will tear a PVC or butyl rubber liner, and smooth out any small hollows or slight rises in the floor and sides. To finish off, line the hole with old carpet or sacking to protect the lining material. If you intend to concrete, then finish off with a thin layer of sand, approximately 13mm/½in thick, to act as a binding layer.

– TOP-UPS AND OVERFLOWS –

A severe drop in water level in a garden pool or pond could result in excess exposure of the pool sides to weathering and considerable problems for any fish and plants; it is therefore advisable to incorporate some form of automatic top-up system.

Such a system usually comprises a top-up chamber fed by a mains water inlet and controlled by a simple ball valve (similar in principle to those used in lavatory cisterns) set to the desired level (see above right).

The opposite side of this problem is excess water, which can also cause damage through erosion of pool and pond sides and banks. The best solution to this is to build an overflow system into the side. The size of the pipe used depends on the size of your pond or pool, but as a general rule 20sq m/215sq ft of surface water needs a 7.5cm/3in diameter

pipe. A surface area larger than this will need at least a 10cm/4in pipe. Make sure that the pipe is inserted into the side of the feature at a point lower than any part of the bank, and run the pipe away at an angle no less than 1:80. Ideally, the excess water should run into a ditch protected with concrete to prevent erosion.

– POOL AND POND TYPES –

The easiest types of pond or pool to install are prefabricated in rigid fiberglass and are available in a good range of shapes and sizes. Most incorporate a molded shelf round the sides for waterside plants to stand on. To install one of these, all you need do is excavate a hole of the same shape, but slightly larger, and then gently lower the mold into the hole, first making sure that all sharp stones have been removed and that there is an insulating layer of sand to hold the mold firmly in position (see bottom left).

PVC and butyl liners

Pool liners are available in either flexible PVC or the more expensive and extremely long-lasting butyl material. Because it is expensive, care should be taken when calculating the amount needed. Unless it is manufactured as one piece, it is impossible to join successfully if you make a mistake.

The length of liner you need will be equal to the length of your pool or pond plus twice the maximum depth. The width comprises the maximum width plus twice the maximum depth. If the liner material is stretchable, there is no need to make allowances for ledges and contours. Prepare the hole as has already been described, taking extra care that there are no sharp objects or stones likely to cause damage. Lay the lining material

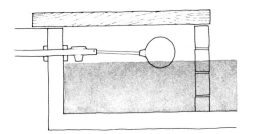

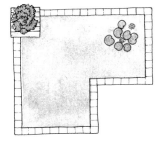

Top-up system
Where water loss is a problem, a top-up system will help to maintain a constant water level. A simple ball valve, like those used for toilet cisterns, set to the required level, will allow the pool to be topped up automatically (top). This arrangement can be attractively concealed beneath a simple wood and brick platform and disguised with plants in pots or baskets (above).

Overflow system
An effective overflow system will help to prevent damage to the pool sides and surrounds from erosion. A pipe inserted into the side and set at a gradient of no less than 1:80 should run into a concrete-lined ditch. If this is not possible, consult your local water authority for permission to run excess water into the nearest storm water pipe.

round the excavated hole, ensuring that there is an even amount of excess right round the outside and weight this down with smooth boulders or bricks. Then start to fill the hole using a pipe – the weight of the water will pull the liner into shape. When the pool has filled to the desired level, cut away any excess liner leaving about 30cm/12in to tuck into the soil and disguise with plants or boulders.

Concrete lining

Concrete is an extremely strong and watertight lining material provided it is properly mixed and handled, and can look most effective when used for features such as formal pools and watercourses. To set properly, concrete needs the right conditions, which means measuring materials carefully when mixing – never rely on guesswork – and keeping all the ingredients clean and free from soil or other garden debris. If the cement powder is lumpy, use it only if you can crumble it back into a fine consistency between your fingers. If it refuses to crumble or is damp, then don't use it – the resulting concrete will be sub-standard and inadequate. As a rule of thumb, the water used in mixing should be pure enough to drink. One of the mistakes many novices make is to add extra water to the concrete mixture to keep it workable after it has been mixed. The effect of doing this is to upset the chemical balance of the concrete and to weaken its basic structure.

To calculate the amount of concrete for a pool, add the surface area of the sides to that of the base and multiply the result by whatever thickness you intend to lay – usually about 15cm/6in. It is safer to overestimate slightly rather than run short, since small pools or ponds should

be covered in a single pouring to prevent uneven drying and cracking. Even large areas should be covered in no more than two pourings. If the area is small enough you can mix up the concrete by hand, otherwise hire a concrete mixer from a local store or order a delivery of ready-mixed. This last option is the most expensive and your estimate of quantity needs to be very accurate. Also, you will have to have all the preparatory work at just the right stage before the truck arrives, and access to the site cleared.

Before any actual work starts, assemble all the necessary tools and materials – ballast (coarse aggregate or gravel), cement and water – to complete the whole job in one session. Begin by covering the surface area of the excavation with 19mm/¾in chicken wire tied together with steel ties. Make sure the wire is in good condition and showing no signs of rust. Start concreting in the morning when the weather is dry but not too hot, otherwise the concrete will dry too quickly. Avoid, too, concreting in wet, frosty or freezing conditions.

Laying concrete

Make up a strong mix of concrete by using volume proportions of one part cement to three parts sand to six of ballast. Use a bucket to calculate your ingredients and a plywood board to mix on, never on an asphalt drive or paving, which is difficult to clean afterwards. Have a tarpaulin or plastic sheet handy, large enough to cover your work completely, in case the weather turns bad.

Mix the dry ingredients until they are evenly distributed and you can detect no color difference, and then add water until the mix reaches an oatmeallike consistency. At this stage you can use anti-

Concrete lining

Once the site has been excavated, the inside should be covered with chicken wire and then a stiff concrete mix worked into it, making sure the wire is completely covered. Angling the sides of the excavation about 20° from the perpendicular will help to prevent the concrete slipping. At the top of the pool sides, the concrete should be recessed into the bank with a notch for a neat finish (see below).

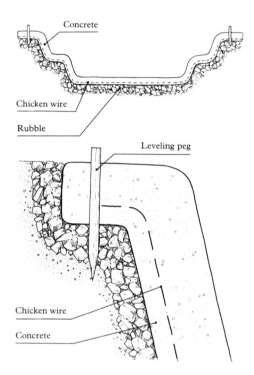

Recessing the concrete

A notch approximately 7.5cm/3in deep at the top edge of the pool sides will recess the concrete neatly into the bank. Remember to remove the leveling pegs before the concrete is dry, and smooth the surface to a good finish using a float. The concrete will settle slightly to fill the holes left by the leveling pegs.

frost, waterproofing and any coloring additives you wish. When you are satisfied with the consistency, take a concreting trowel and apply the mix to the sides and base of your pool or pond in about a 15cm/6in layer, taking care to work it into the chicken wire and making sure that it is completely covered. If the concrete mix is stiff enough, it should not start to slip down, making the base thicker than the top. Angling the sides of the excavation at about 20° from the perpendicular should make wooden forms unnecessary. When you reach the top of the edge, recess the concrete into the bank with a 7.5cm/3in notch (see bottom left) and remove the bank leveling peg before the concrete is dry. Finally, use the float to bring the surface to a fine, smooth finish.

The longer the concrete takes to dry the stronger it will be, and in hot weather you should cover it with polyethylene to slow down the process a little. Concrete will continue to harden throughout its life (even under water), but you can fill your pool or pond with water as soon as the initial hardening has taken place and it is dry to the touch. Empty and refill at least two or three times to flush out the lime content in the concrete, since it is harmful to both fish and aquatic plants; it is a good idea to leave the pond for about three months before stocking just to make sure the last of the lime has been dissolved.

Clay puddling
Liners and concrete simply are not practicable for large ponds, and these will have to be sealed using a clay puddling technique instead. The natural clay lining the pond or pool should be reasonably damp and malleable, and where this material does not naturally occur, it has to be introduced. There is a special type of absorptive bentonite clay, marketed as Volclay. It is applied dry to the substrate in a layer 5 to 7.5cm/2 to 3in thick, and then worked into the surface with a rototiller. Once wet, it forms an excellent seal. With natural clay, small areas can be worked using flat, sturdy wooden boards, or tampers. Waterproof rubber boots, however, are just as effective. But with large ponds it is more usual to use excavating machinery both to apply and puddle the clay to the sides and bottom. To achieve a satisfactory waterproof bond you will need to build up thin layers to a minimum overall thickness of about 15cm/6in.

Clay puddling is hard work, but it is a method that has been used for hundreds of years for maintaining village ponds.

Swimming pools
Swimming pools are constructed on much the same lines as concrete-lined pools described earlier but are, of course, on a far larger scale. Swimming pools also require the addition of pumping, filtering and heating services and are, traditionally, tiled. Cost and upheaval are also greater than with an ordinary pond or pool, and while it is possible to install one yourself it is advisable to buy the components in kit form from a company that can provide full back-up facilities. The plumbing, electrical and heating components need to be installed by experts, since they are difficult for an amateur to tackle and potentially dangerous if installed incorrectly. Large excavating machinery is almost always necessary (see p. 127) and soil generally has to be removed from the site, so do remember to allow for the cost of this and to plan for adequate access.

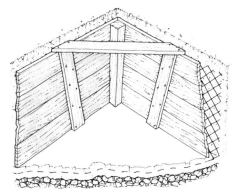

Concrete forms
A good stiff concrete mix and sloping sides well covered in chicken wire should provide adequate adhesion for your concrete lining, but, if necessary, wooden forms can be built in order to keep the concrete in place. Position the forms round the sides of the excavation, allowing a sufficient gap for the chicken wire and concrete layer. Remove the wood when the concrete is dry.

RUNNING WATER

In the majority of cases, waterfalls, streams, watercourses, and certainly fountains, will be artificially fed by an electric pump that recycles the water from the lowest point back up to the highest. Wherever the depth of water allows, a submersible pump is more economical to run and less trouble to maintain, and can provide an output of up to 4500 litres/1000 gallons per hour with a head of water (the height of the cascade above the water level of the pond or pool) of about 1m/3ft 3in. As the head of water increases so the output decreases, while length of pipe, bore and any bends will also affect performance.

It is important to choose a pump capable of handling your particular feature easily, especially when using a single pump to serve both a waterfall and fountain, for example, by incorporating a T-piece in the outlet pipe. No pump will give good service if it is pushed to its operating limits all the time and manufacturers always give recommended maximum output for a particular model. If you are in any doubt, consult your stockist before you buy.

Installation is straightforward and involves concealing the pump and connecting the outlet pipe to the top of your waterfall or base of your fountain and then running the armored cable provided to the nearest electrical point. The cable should be installed by a qualified electrician and, for safety's sake, buried underground where there is no danger of it being accidentally sliced by a spade or shovel. For extra protection, run the cable inside plastic conduit. All plugs must be waterproof and properly fused.

– FOUNTAINS AND WATER SCULPTURES –
With fountains you must choose a pump capacity to suit the size of spray you want – too large and you lose a lot of water from spillage or from the wind catching it; too small and the effect is simply inadequate. The best arrangement to overcome this problem is a simple flow valve to regulate the water spout.

To install a basic display fountain all you need is a length of plastic tubing of the correct diameter to connect to your pump and a fountain nozzle or jet available in a wide range of configurations. Connect the tubing with clamps and support the nozzle or jet just clear of the water's surface. For something more elaborate, the tubing can be connected to a pipe emerging from an ornament or built into a water sculpture.

For small patios or households with young children, a bubble fountain is ideal, since the water reservoir can be concealed underground with the water emerging as bubbles over a set of cobbles or an old millstone. You will need to sink your reservoir into the ground and conceal the pump, positioning the water spout at ground level in the center of your water feature. As with any fountain, take care that water does not splash over the sides of the containment area or you will have serious water loss and possible damage to surrounding surfaces.

As a general rule, the dimensions of the pool or hidden reservoir should not be less than twice the height of the fountain jet.

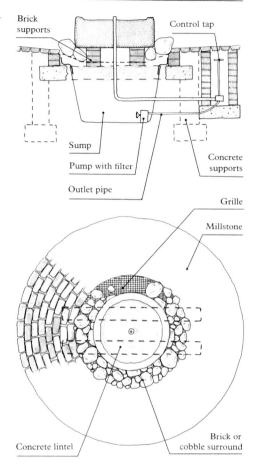

Installing a bubble fountain
A bubble fountain is easy to construct and install by concealing a submersible pump and filter in an underground reservoir (top). Water is pumped up through a small outlet pipe concealed by a stone, such as a millstone, or pebbles at ground level, and runs back through a hidden grille to be recycled. The sump below ground level can be butyl or concrete lined. Use bricks on concrete lintels to support the millstone in position, as can be seen in the overhead view (above).

– WATERFALLS –

Trial and error is the only successful way to construct a waterfall, experimenting with different boulders, spouts or saucers until the effect is right. For this reason, do not fix anything permanently in place until you are completely satisfied with the overall effect.

Begin by planning the gradient of your waterfall – perhaps as part of a rockery, a series of cascades or even a flow of water down the face of a wall. As well as checking that your pump can handle the height, the actual surface the water will be flowing over should be made waterproof. In the example of a classic rocky waterfall, this means installing a series of saucers or pools or a strong butyl lining concealed behind the natural rocks. Take care that each pool or saucer is capable of holding water before spilling over to the next level and that they are straight.

There are two common problems with waterfalls, both of which are easily solved. First, the outlet pipe often allows water to seep out between the pipe and concrete. This occurs if the pipe has been brought through the side of the top cascade. Instead, position the pipe over the top of the cascade (see below) and you will have no further problem. Second, surface tension makes it difficult to form a proper cascade of water – it just dribbles down the rock face, clinging to the surface. The easy way round this is to incorporate a ledge in the top lip of the fall that propels the water out and over. The lip can be built of timber or, even better, clear fiberglass, which as it is completely transparent will not intrude.

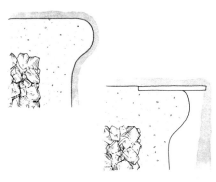

Improving a waterfall
To prevent water from a waterfall or cascade flowing down the back of an overhang, insert a small clear fiberglass lip to lift the water away from the back wall. As well as improving the fall and creating a curtain of water, the fiberglass will be virtually invisible to all but the closest inspection.

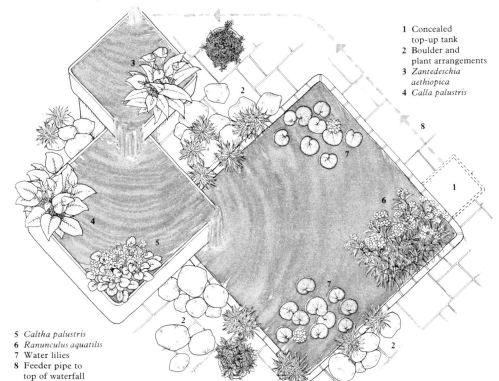

1 Concealed top-up tank
2 Boulder and plant arrangements
3 *Zantedeschia aethiopica*
4 *Calla palustris*
5 *Caltha palustris*
6 *Ranunculus aquatilis*
7 Water lilies
8 Feeder pipe to top of waterfall

Formal waterfall feature
Old sinks, troughs or, indeed, any watertight square or rectangular containers can be used to make an excellent formal waterfall feature. Arrange containers of varying sizes at different levels so that they slightly overlap each other. This should allow water to spill gently from one to another before entering a formal pool at the bottom of the arrangement. In the bottom of the pool you will need to install a submersible pump to recycle the water up to the top again. Large boulders and pebbles interspersed with potted plants can be arranged around the waterfall to help integrate it into its setting. If the flow of water is gentle enough, water lilies and other aquatic plants can be installed, too.

– STREAMS AND WATERCOURSES –
When constructing a stream or water-course, it should be built in the same way as a pool or pond (see pp. 126-31) by paying strict attention to keeping the banks level. Mark out and prepare in the same way and then set up a 1.2m/4ft leveling post at the start of the stream. Place a second post 3m/10ft away in line with the direction of the stream, making sure it is level with the first post by checking with a straightedge and level. Next, position a third post at the far end of the stream and then stretch a length of fishing line between all three to ensure they are in a straight line. It is important that the line does not actually touch the second post (leave a gap of about 1mm), otherwise it may deflect it and produce a misleading reading.

Next you will need to make a T-shaped rod – its height should be from the top of the post to the ground plus the depth of the proposed stream excavation (usually about 60cm/24in). Now you can use the rod as a guide to excavation, making sure that as you dig down it remains level with the line at the top (see below).

This system is only really suitable for relatively straight streams and water-courses. For streams with twists and bends, you will need the help of an optical level, a professional instrument that is available by rental. Never build a stream with a sloping bed hoping to increase the water flow: it will simply collect at the bottom and wait to be pumped back to the beginning again. To cope with a sloping site, you need to build a series of level weirs and pools along the course of the stream, which will allow the water to collect and build up before spilling over to the next lowest level. Streams and watercourses can be lined and finished according to the instructions for pools (see pp. 126-31).

Leveling a stream
To ensure that a stream is level, bank to bank, construct a T-shaped measuring rod of the correct height and use it as a guide to excavation, measuring from the bank to the center of the stream bed using a straightedge and level. Use a wooden peg to mark the exact level and excavate accordingly.

Leveling a stream along its length
To maintain a constant level along a stream's course, set up two posts (about 3m/10ft apart) at the start of the course and in line with the proposed direction of the stream. Check that the posts are level using a straightedge and level and then set the height of a third post at the far end of the stream using a length of fishing line. Make a T-shaped rod, measuring from the top of the posts to the depth of the proposed excavation. When the top of the rod is at the same height as the fishing line, the stream is at the correct depth.

Step 1

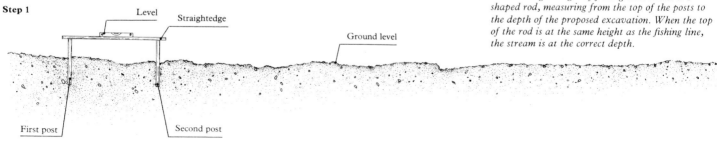

Level
Straightedge
Ground level
First post
Second post

Step 2

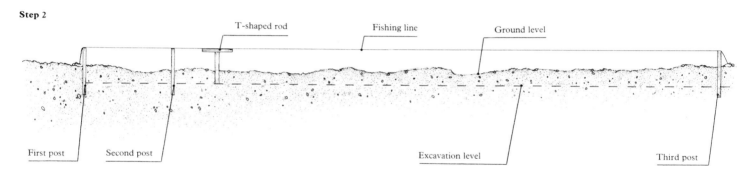

T-shaped rod
Fishing line
Ground level
First post
Second post
Excavation level
Third post

MAKING A BOG GARDEN

You may have a naturally damp area in the garden that can easily be turned into a bog garden. Badly drained, clay-based sites are best, as are areas where the water table is naturally close to the surface. If these conditions do not apply, however, you can create a bog garden using a perforated butyl liner, as described below.

The ideal site for your bog garden should be sheltered with a little, but not total, shade. Make sure it is not too close to tree roots, which will tend to drain most of the moisture from the soil.

– INSTALLATION AND CONSTRUCTION –
In small plots the container-type of bog garden is easy to install and maintain. Old stone sinks, for example, make excellent mini bog gardens, complete with drainage holes, and can be set at different levels with water allowed to flow from one to another. Old barrels can be used in the same way once you have drilled three or four drainage holes in each one.

Constructing a larger bog garden is no more difficult. Excavate the desired area to a depth of approximately 35cm/14in and cover it with a large sheet of PVC or butyl pool lining material. Anchor the material in place with large, smooth boulders that will not tear the material and then puncture the bottom of the liner with small drainage holes – about one hole per square meter – to allow some of the water to escape. The idea is to retain most of the water with about 5 to 7.5cm/2 to 3in standing on top of the soil itself.

Because bog gardens need to be so poorly drained you will have to make some allowance for the water level to rise and fall as rainfall fluctuates. In a naturally wet and boggy site drainage will already exist and a fairly even level of moisture can be maintained. If, however, you have constructed the garden along the lines described above, you will have to provide some form of overflow system. If your bog area adjoins a pond, a few 13mm/½in diameter holes in the dividing wall should give adequate top-up and drainage facilities during periods of excessively dry and wet weather. For this system to work, the bog garden should be not more than 10 to 15 per cent of the total surface area of the pond – otherwise the flow may work in reverse.

Where there is no pond or other water nearby, you will have to provide overflow facilities to a ditch or other drainage system. And should the area start to dry out, bog gardens will need topping up with water from a hose. The most convenient way of doing this is to lay a section of plastic pipe in the bottom of the bog but on top of the rubber lining material. Punch holes in the pipe at about 60cm/24in intervals and leave the end of the pipe exposed above the ground where it can be attached to a pipe. The exposed end of pipe can be disguised when you come to plant out the bog garden. This watering technique is best, since it more closely mimics the way a natural bog garden is fed.

Simple bog garden
Old barrels make excellent small bog gardens, particularly when several can be sunk into the ground and surrounded by pebbles. Drill three or four drainage holes in the bottom of each barrel and saturate the soil with water before planting. One or two striking moisture-loving plants can be planted in each barrel to create interesting and unusual effects in even the smallest patio or garden.

Pebbles

Free-draining soil

Drainage holes

Crocks

INSTALLING A BRIDGE

Bridges are generally constructed of wood, concrete or stone and can be as simple as a single log, concrete slab or a flat piece of stone well secured to both banks of a stream or watercourse. As has already been explained (see pp. 64-9), bridges need to be wide enough to cross comfortably – at least 60cm/24in – but preferably wide enough so lawn mowers or wheelbarrows can be taken across, too. Single-span bridges are the simplest to build, and about 2.4m/8ft is the limit you can stretch a span before additional sup-port is required in the form of piers driven into the bed of the stream or watercourse. A special pile-driving machine will be necessary for this.

– WOODEN BRIDGE –

Concrete and stone bridges tend to be difficult and expensive to construct and you will almost certainly require the services of a professional to carry the project through. Lumber construction, however, can be equally sturdy and extremely attractive and is more within the scope of a skilled do-it-yourselfer. You must bear in mind, though, that a wood-built bridge will need more maintenance and has a shorter life, perhaps only 10 to 15 years. All lumbers used must be treated with preservative and any in contact with the water should be of oak, elm or a comparable hardwood.

Stone bridge
A simple stone or granite slab, well secured in concrete on either bank, makes a fine bridge across an informal stream. Disguise the concrete footings with boulders and plants.

Japanese-style wooden bridge
A very effective oriental-style bridge can be built using simple lumber scaffolding. Position 15 × 15cm/6 × 6in support posts so that they stand about 15cm/6in above the proposed water level to form a zigzag pattern. Bolt joists of 7.5 × 15cm/3 × 6in lumber to the posts and nail down a series of wooden planks in pairs.

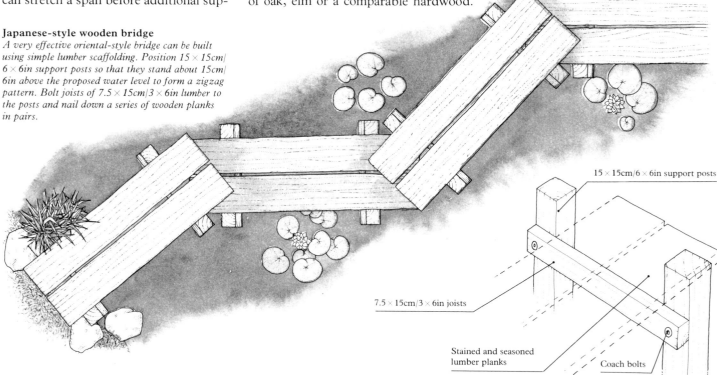

15 × 15cm/6 × 6in support posts

7.5 × 15cm/3 × 6in joists

Stained and seasoned lumber planks

Coach bolts

The wood will need treating annually with preservative and all exposed surfaces scoured with a wire brush twice a year to remove algae growth, which can become slippery underfoot. Planking can be covered with chicken wire to provide a nonslip surface, but it is not particularly hard wearing and, depending on the level of traffic, may need renewing every 12 to 18 months.

A single-span wooden bridge can be simply constructed by driving in and securing joist supporting posts on both banks, making sure they are level by stretching a rigid line between the two and checking them with a level. Solid 10×10cm/4×4in wooden joists are then fastened to these, spanning the water and covered with planking at right angles to provide a sound surface to walk on. Planking is generally 5×10cm/2×4in or 5×15cm/2×6in and secured to the joists using good quality 9cm/$3\frac{1}{2}$in screws or 10cm/4in nails. The posts used to support the joists need to be at least 10×15cm/4×6in.

For safety, a handrail or balustrade should be installed. This should not be less than 1m/3ft 3in high, sturdily constructed and firmly fixed. If you have young children, you may want to fill the space between the supporting beams with chicken wire. The top rail should provide a firm, smooth grip and be made from 5×5cm/2×2in planks or 7.5cm/3in diameter poles – never use cheap rustic poles, which rot too quickly. All softwoods should be protected against weathering with a regular application of nontoxic preservative. Check with your supplier that the preservative will not adversely affect plants or fish.

If you need to install supporting piers for bridges longer than 2.4m/8ft, these will have to be driven in by a purpose-built machine available for rent from specialist suppliers. The piers must be a minimum of 10×10cm/4×4in but 15×15cm/6×6in is preferable. Do not sharpen supporting lumber to a point, since it will tend to twist and move off-center when being driven in if it encounters large stones or boulders.

– CONCRETE BRIDGE –

The easiest way to construct a concrete bridge over a stream or ditch is to build a concrete channel, or culvert, as the support for the structure. Care must be taken that the size of the culvert is sufficient to handle the volume of water during high water periods, otherwise your bridge could be severely affected by erosion.

Before undertaking this type of work try to assess realistically your ability to see it through and, if in doubt, bring in specialist assistance. The first step is to divert or dam the stream while the bridge is being built and then to install a concrete block on the stream bed on which to seat the culvert. Next, the culvert, which can be bought complete or made by a specialist company to your specification, needs to be lowered carefully into position and the sides backfilled with rubble or the sides formed and filled with concrete. The whole structure should then be faced with brick or stone to retain the rubble or just to give an attractive finish to the concrete. If the bridge is for foot traffic only, it should be covered with a 7.5cm/3in slab or the equivalent thickness of concrete mix. You can then use any paving material you wish to finish off. Twice this thickness of reinforced concrete is required for vehicular traffic, but obtain specialist advice.

Concrete and culvert bridge
A culvert, or large concrete pipe, makes an easy-to-install support for a concrete bridge over a stream or watercourse. Lower the culvert carefully onto a bed of concrete and backfill with rubble or, using wooden forms, concrete. This should then be faced with brick or stone to create an attractive finish. If the bridge is to be subjected to heavy use, strengthen the top with a 15cm/6in layer of reinforced concrete.

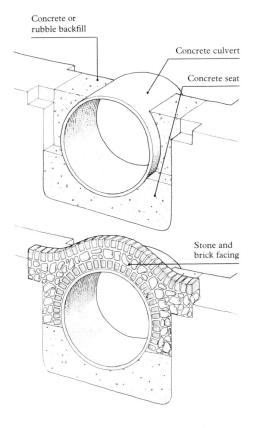

Concrete or rubble backfill

Concrete culvert

Concrete seat

Stone and brick facing

LAYING HARD SURFACES

◆

There are two main types of hard-surface paving materials: unit paving, which covers bricks, stone blocks, paving slabs and natural stones, and continuous paving, which usually refers to a mixture of granular materials such as concrete or pebbles. Choosing between these two types will depend on how you intend to use the area to be paved. If it is mainly for pedestrian traffic then a relatively brittle material such as concrete paving slabs can be used. If, however, it will be subjected to vehicular traffic, then poured concrete reinforced with steel rods may be a better choice.

Consider other uses you may put the paved area to before making a final decision. Unit paving makes it easier to leave gaps for planting out small areas, while continuous paving is a better option for a children's playing area or anywhere garden furniture is to stand. Color, texture, size and tone all come into it too, and a variety of materials can be used in a design if the elements are chosen with care. The best policy, however, is usually simplicity, so do not use too many different types or an overly elaborate pattern.

As with any material intended for outdoor use, check that bricks, tiles and paving are of the right type to withstand the effects of frost and rain: porous bricks, for example, may flake or crack in a severe frost, and special-quality paving bricks only should be used in these circumstances.

– UNIT PAVING –

The long-term success of unit paving depends on good preparation of the base, and it is important to excavate all boggy or crumbly, friable organic soil from the site, since this material lacks stability. If necessary, backfill with ballast or rubble to bring the area up to the correct level. The finished, paved level will inevitably reflect the final level of the base, so double check that all excavation work is accurate. If you are in any doubt about the suitability of the subsoil, seek the advice of a qualified expert.

You can calculate the required depth of excavation by adding together the thicknesses of the different layers and subtracting the total from your desired finished level. The bottom-most level will consist of a 7.5 to 15cm/3 to 6in layer of rubble. The thickness of this depends on the paving material being used – large stone or concrete slabs, for example, will require only 7.5cm/3in because the size of the slab helps to distribute the weight when walked on. Bricks or stone blocks, on the other hand, need the deeper 15cm/6in of rubble to support the same weight of traffic. On top of the rubble comes a 2.5cm/1in layer of sand and a 2.5cm/1in layer of mortar. You then must allow about 7.5 to 10cm/3 to 4in depending on the thickness of your paving material. For a really long-lasting finish, the rubble has to be well compacted and it may be worthwhile hiring a roller or tamping machine.

Another point to bear in mind when

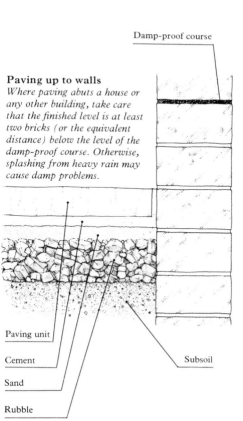

Draining a paved surface
Paved surfaces should be sloped to drain away from the house wherever possible. If this can't be done, a gutter should be constructed to carry water away from the base of the building where it could cause damp problems (below). The height of the edging units will determine the degree of slope, which should be about 1:100.

Damp-proof course

Paving up to walls
Where paving abuts a house or any other building, take care that the finished level is at least two bricks (or the equivalent distance) below the level of the damp-proof course. Otherwise, splashing from heavy rain may cause damp problems.

Paving unit

Cement

Sand

Rubble

Subsoil

laying unit paving is the proximity of your surface to the house or any other substantial building. It is important that the finished level of the paving is at least two bricks (or the equivalent distance) below the level of any damp-proof course (DPC). Otherwise, the DPC may be breached and dampness penetrate inside the building. Also, to help keep water away from walls, wherever possible the surface should slope slightly away from the building, but if this is not possible it will be necessary to install a drainage gully running alongside the wall. And, from a purely aesthetic point of view, paving laid hard up against a brick wall should align with an existing level of brickwork.

Technique

With all forms of unit paving, you should lay the edging units first, set in concrete, and then allow this to harden for 24 hours. The level of the edging determines the direction and degree of drainage slope, which should be about 1:100. This is achieved by preparing the foundation levels as already described and positioning the edging units at the correct level at the highest point – preferably near the house. Determine the position of the opposite edging units with the aid of a space tumbler and level (see below) at the lowest point of the surface.

After the edging has hardened, mix up and layer your mortar bed to the correct thickness (2.5cm/1in) using a mix of 6:1 sand and cement, making sure that it is not too wet. Knock in your bricks or slabs using a heavy, level piece of wood and a hammer, allowing for a 10mm/⅓in gap between each unit for grouting. Leave the mortar to dry for 48 hours and then brush dry grouting into the joints using a mix of 2:1 fine silver sand and cement. Both the paving surface and the grouting must be completely dry or it will stain the bricks or slabs. Firm the grouting into the joints using a blunt piece of wood and repeat. Moisture in the air will set the mixture, but if the weather is exceptionally dry, dampen the joints slightly using a watering can with a fine rose.

– CONTINUOUS PAVING –

To lay continuous paving you should prepare a good, sound base as described for unit paving and observe the same guidelines for drainage. First, set in your edging of brick, curbstone or lumber as required, or position a temporary framework of wooden formwork for a plain concrete finish. Next, mix and pour on your concrete and then smooth the surface roughly with a stout board, such as

Mixing materials
A mixture of paving materials can be used very effectively to create a more varied look around a water feature. Here, brick edging separates concrete paving to make an attractive checkerboard design. Small raised pools, using old stone sinks, look completely at home.

Laying unit paving
Unit paving needs a stable, level base, excavated to the correct level to allow for the appropriate layers of base materials and the final thickness of the slabs or bricks themselves. Well-compacted rubble should be dressed with a 2.5cm/1in layer of sand, topped with the same thickness of cement. The type of paving material used will determine the thickness of rubble, which can be compacted using a hired vibrating machine.

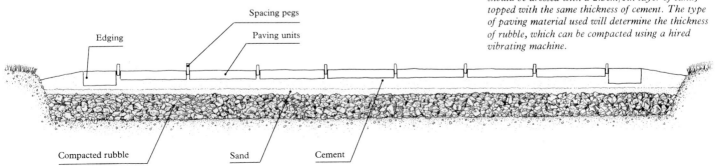

Edging · Spacing pegs · Paving units · Compacted rubble · Sand · Cement

a scaffold plank. To achieve a fine concrete finish, tamp the board to the edging in a continuous chopping motion. Be careful not to overtamp or the cement mixture will begin to separate causing weaknesses in the basic structure. Allow the mixture to harden slightly for about four hours and then render smooth using a float. The float produces a surface too smooth if immediately adjacent to a pond or pool, so brush with a soft broom to texture the surface or brush in some aggregate, such as fine gravel.

In areas prone to winter frosts, it is a good idea to include a frost-proofing additive when mixing concrete (see pp. 126-31) and, as a precaution, always cover a newly laid area with a sheet of polyethylene or a tarpaulin if there is any risk of rain or frost before the concrete has completely hardened.

Concrete finishes

Concrete in itself is not particularly exciting or attractive, but there are many ways it can be dressed up and decorated. Apart from the brushed finish already mentioned, it can be colored with a special additive applied to the dry concrete mix. Stone, marble chippings or fine shingle applied to the wet surface can also be used to produce a speckled

mosaic effect. If you like the appearance of exposed aggregate, brush the surface with a soft broom about six to eight hours after laying and then hose to expose the aggregate used in the mixture. Another alternative is to mark out areas of concrete with lines of bricks – an excellent device to link a paved area to a brick-edged pool or pond.

– Unusual Paving Materials –
Interesting and original effects can be created around a pool or pond area using less conventional paving materials. Stone and Belgian blocks about 13 or 25sq cm/ 5 or 10 sq in, more usually employed in road construction, can be bought second-hand and make an excellent and hard-wearing surface, especially when laid in patterns or used in conjunction with smaller, unit paving. A soft and inexpensive alternative to traditional paving is log rings, which need to be well treated with preservative, either set in concrete or laid on a soil bed and surrounded by turf or forest bark mulch. The log rings should be cut from hardwood and be at least 15cm/6in thick. Old railroad ties are yet another economical and durable surfacing material and combine well with other, more traditional materials, such as concrete or bricks.

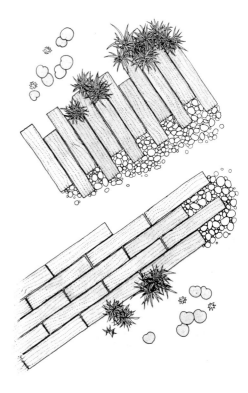

Wood paths
Old railroad ties make excellent wood paths when laid directly on the soil in a natural, woodland-style water garden. They can be laid side by side and slightly staggered for an informal look, or positioned end to end.

Making a pebble beach
A pebble beach will help to soften and protect the edges of a butyl-lined pool. Run the liner well up a gently sloping bank and then lay irregular-shaped pebbles over it to form the beach effect. You can create a strong visual link with the surrounding paving by setting areas of pebbles into it. Run the pebbles into the water for a more unified look.

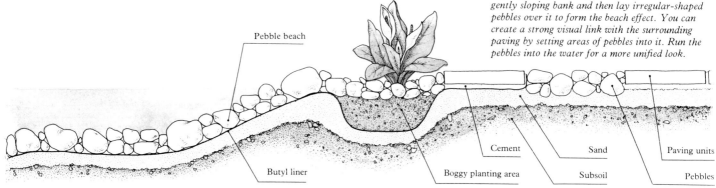

Pebble beach

Butyl liner

Boggy planting area

Cement

Sand

Subsoil

Paving units

Pebbles

WOODEN DECKS

◆

Apart from being reasonably simple to construct, wooden decking has a fine, natural appearance and looks good in a wide variety of settings. It really comes into its own, however, with a sloping or very uneven site, where the construction of a concrete patio would involve making a large retaining wall and then backfilling to provide a level surface for paving.

– TYPES OF DECK –

For the averagely skilled home do-it-yourselfer, a ground-level deck is the simplest to undertake. A deck raised high off the ground should be built by a skilled professional, as should any decks built on wet or unstable ground, like that found near a natural bog garden, for example (see p. 135).

If the ground is firm and stable, a low-level deck can be installed using metal fence-support spikes that prevent any part of the wooden supporting posts coming into contact with the ground. These posts should be either 10×10cm/4×4in or 15×15cm/6×6in depending on the distance being spanned by the bearer beams, which should be 7.5×10cm/3×4in to 10×15cm/4×6in. The wood used for the actual walking surface should be 2.5×5cm/1×2in, 2.5×7.5cm/1×3in or even 2.5×10cm/1×4in, with slightly beveled edges for a neat finish. You can lay the decking planks either in straight, parallel courses or in more attractive zigzag patterns; but remember that every time the wood changes direction it will need to be nailed down and this will mean providing supporting beams at those points.

A lumber deck adjoining the house can be supported on one side by a horizontal wall bearer, attached to the house with masonry bolts (expanding rawlbolts). Joists can then be extended from the wall bearer to a sturdy support post fixed to a concrete footing at least $60 \times 60 \times 60$cm/$24 \times 24 \times 24$in using a 2.5cm/1in reinforcing bar as a dowel (see right). Free-standing decks should not be built more than 1m/3ft 3in off the ground unless you are an experienced carpenter. Support posts must not be more than 1.8m/6ft apart and horizontal joists between 1 to 1.2m/3 to 4ft apart. Let the decking planks overhang the bearers by about 7.5cm/3in to disguise the supporting structure. Trim the ends of the decking only when the deck is completely finished to ensure a perfectly straight and neat series of cuts.

All lumber used in any type of deck construction should have been pressure treated with preservative. No further preservative need then be applied. Although more prone to splintering than hardwoods, softwoods are generally used for decks because hardwoods are extremely expensive. For a long-lasting and neat finish use only galvanized nails and screws (brass is expensive, but looks best) and countersink all screwheads to prevent accidents.

Where a safety rail is required with a raised deck, use extended support posts to provide the uprights and sturdy coach-bolts to attach the horizontal planks. For the top rail, rounded wood gives a good finish, and it should have a diameter of 7.5cm/3in.

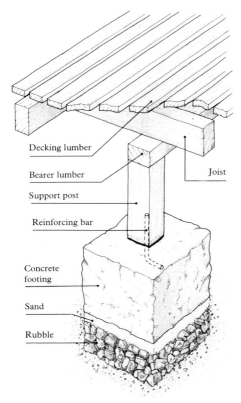

Decking lumber

Bearer lumber

Joist

Support post

Reinforcing bar

Concrete footing

Sand

Rubble

Supporting a wooden deck
Low-level decks are not difficult to install on firm, stable ground using 10×10cm/4×4in or 15×15cm/6×6in wooden support posts driven into metal fencing spikes or fixed into concrete footings at least $60 \times 60 \times 60$cm/$12 \times 12 \times 12$in, and using a 2.5cm/1in reinforcing bar as a dowel. These posts are spanned by bearer beams usually between 7.5×10cm/3×4in and 10×15cm/4×6in, depending on the distance between posts. Bearer beams can also be fitted to the side of the house if necessary.

GARDEN LIGHTING

Water and electricity are a potentially lethal partnership and your primary consideration when installing lighting anywhere outdoors must be safety, especially with lights or cables actually in or near a pool or pond. Although the price may be high, it makes sense to select only the best-quality fittings, which should be well made and sturdy and recommended for outdoor use, with weatherproof moldings, rubberized cables and sealed gaskets. Beware of cheap, badly fitting components and inferior materials. A large garden center or specialist pool and hot tub supplier should be able to advise you on the suitability of a particular light fitting and assess your plans from a practical point of view.

The lighting principles already discussed (see pp. 76-80) should give you some idea of the types of effect you can achieve when using thoughtfully positioned lights in conjunction with a water feature. It is, however, important that when planning the best position for spot and floodlights that you conceal them efficiently – a beautifully lit pool at night, for example, is not much good if your garden bristles with unattractive hardware in the cold light of day. Some lights, such as lamp posts standing as high as 2.4m/8ft, are, of course, ornamental and meant to be seen in daylight.

– INSTALLATION AND SUITABILITY –

Unless you are an experienced do-it-yourselfer and have tackled electrical installation projects before, you are strongly advised not to attempt to install your own outdoor and pool lighting. Instead, contact a few experienced electrical contractors and have them quote for the job. Ask for their advice on the type of cable, safety features and fittings they would recommend and then try to assess their competence – don't make your decision solely on the grounds of the cheapest quotation.

Lighting around a pool
External floodlights and spotlights can be remarkably effective at illuminating particular areas of the water garden. Spiked floods and spots can be anchored securely in the ground and disguised with boulders and plants. Or use concealed well lights, which sit flush with the surface of the ground, for unobtrusive up-lighting.

FLOODLIGHTS
A series of floods, each with its own ground spike, can be run from a single transformer.

SPOTLIGHTS
Single spotlights are useful for highlighting specific features, paths and bridges.

WELL LIGHTS
These lights are fitted with toughened safety glass and below-ground drainage should be provided by a bed of gravel.

The power supply for your lights can usually be combined with the services supplying other electrical features, such as pumps and filters, but the power load per cable will have to be assessed: you can't, for example, run an unlimited number of lights or features from a single cable. Light fittings usually vary between 150w to 300w for larger spotlights, and the number your cable can handle is determined both by the power requirements of the lights and the distance the cable has to run – voltage levels drop over long distances and a thicker cable may then be required to accommodate an extra power load. It may be more expensive to install several power cables, but it is certainly worth the cost for the enhanced flexibility and better effects this offers.

When considering the installation of low-voltage underwater lights, you must bear in mind that they need additional transformers to convert the charge and, again, only a couple can be put through a single cable. On balance, then, a single-cable installation may prove to be a false economy in the long run.

Types of cable and installation are also affected by official regulations, and your local electricity authority or electrical contractor should be able to advise you on these. As a general rule, however, all cable for exterior use should be protected by a special plastic conduit and should be buried to a minimum depth of at least 46cm/18in. At this depth it is unlikely to be disturbed by an unwary spade or garden fork. As a less expensive and easier alternative, it is sometimes possible to run a cable along a garden wall close to where it is needed, so long as it can be safely fitted well out of reach. Special fitting clips are available for this and, if possible, tuck the cable into the mortar pointing where it will be slightly recessed and protected from the worst of the weather and accidental damage.

For your extra security and safety, all exterior wiring should be fitted with a residual current-operated circuit breaker, known as an RCB, which detects even a small deviation in the current reaching the earth (somewhere in the region of a mere 30 milliamps) and then cuts the power off automatically.

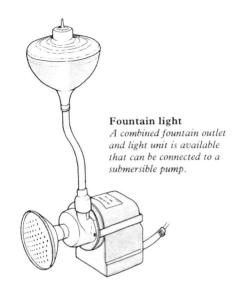

Fountain light
A combined fountain outlet and light unit is available that can be connected to a submersible pump.

Underwater lights
Underwater lights must be low voltage and recommended for pool and pond use. They are particularly attractive used with fountains, cascades and other moving water features, and in swimming pools likely to be used after dark. There is a wide range of fittings, incorporating single or multiple lights run from a single transformer.

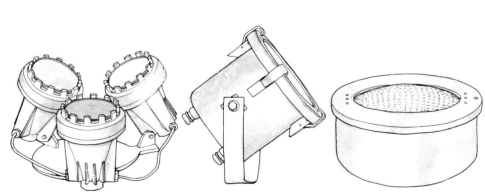

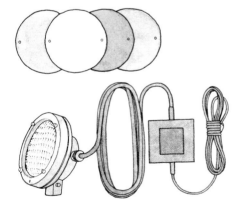

UNDERWATER SPOTLIGHTS
A set of three underwater spots with interchangeable filters.

SINGLE UNDERWATER LAMP
A heavy-duty underwater floodlight for highlighting features from beneath the water.

SWIMMING POOL LIGHT
This type of light should be installed along the pool sides.

PORTABLE POOL LIGHT
This type of portable underwater light has its own integral transformer, which is sited out of the water, and a full set of colored filters.

PLANTS & PLANTING

Water lilies and other floating aquatics should be planted in wire or plastic open baskets, which are then lowered carefully into the water. For larger groups of plants, use an old plastic milk crate as a container. Planting a basket or crate is the same and involves lining it first with turf to help retain the soil, which consists of heavy silty or claylike material topped with stones after planting. This method not only prevents the soil drifting out of the container and polluting the water, but also makes the plants easier to remove and maintain whenever necessary. The topping of stones will also prevent fish disturbing the soil. The combination of plant, basket, soil and stones is heavy, so do take care when lowering the arrangement into the water that you do not disturb the water too much or cause damage to plastic- or rubber-lined ponds and pools. If you have back problems (see pp. 152-3), get somebody to help you to place the container in position rather than risk unnecessary injury.

It is extremely important to place containers at the correct level so that the plants' leaves just float on the surface of the water. In deep water, this may involve propping your baskets and crates up on weighted blocks, which should be large enough to support the container safely without rocking, to achieve just the right depth of planting. If using bricks or concrete blocks, take care not to damage the lining material.

– SOIL TYPES –

If you have heavy clay soil you can treat it with sharp sand to help break down the soil particles. An alkaline soil will be helped by the addition of peat, spent hops and compost – although you will even then never be able to grow avowed lime-haters, such as rhododendrons and azaleas. A free-draining soil such as sand will benefit from being enriched with organic vegetable matter to help retain moisture. Many waterside plants will help to retain moisture in the soil with their root systems and their large leaves, which tend to shade the soil, but it is always a good idea to mulch around them with peat, gravel, chippings or stones to slow down evaporation from the soil surface.

– PLANTING WATERSIDE PLANTS –

Waterside, or bog, plants (see pp. 100-11) are usually planted on the purpose-built ledge of a pool or pond or in the shallow area at the water's edge, depending on the style of your feature. Ledges will need to be back-filled with soil and fronted with large rocks and stones to prevent soil and plants slipping into the water.

Take care that specimens are planted at exactly the same level as they were in the pot or nursery bed and that the ground is not frozen. First, remove the plant from its burlap wrapping, pot or polyethylene container. Measure its root. Then excavate a hole at least four times this size. Remove the topsoil and keep it in a separate pile away from any poorer, deeper soil so that it can be used again after mixing with peat or organic matter. Poorer soil should be discarded.

Before planting, make sure the plant is well watered and that its roots are thoroughly wet, and then slightly break

Plants in baskets
Open plastic baskets are readily available and they are ideal for installing aquatic plants. Line the basket with turf to help retain the soil and then fill with heavy clay soil that will hold moisture well and not crumble away to pollute the water. A topping of small stones helps to keep everything in place and discourages fish from disturbing the plant's roots.

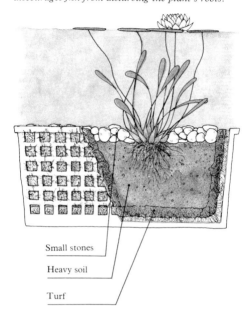

Small stones

Heavy soil

Turf

Planting a waterside shelf
The narrow shelf just under the water's surface will need backfilling with a rich soil mixture and the plant inserted to the same level it had when in its pot. Spread the roots out gently and firm the soil around them. Use rocks or boulders on the edge of the shelf to stop the plant and its soil slipping into the water.

up the sides and bottom of the planting hole with a fork. Lower the plant into its hole, taking great care not to damage the roots and making sure that it comes to rest at exactly its original pot level. Backfill the hole with the enriched topsoil mixture and at this stage you can also add a handful of granular, slow-release fertilizer, providing you ensure that it is well mixed with the soil and does not come into direct contact with the plant's roots. Finally, firm the soil gently round the plant and water it in.

It is important that you carry out this entire procedure in one uninterrupted session: a plant removed for too long from its container will start to suffer damage to the exposed, delicate root fibers, which could kill the plant.

– PLANT CARE –

Water plants need very little maintenance, and this generally consists of removing dead leaves as required and thinning the more vigorous varieties. Sometimes, tall plants in exposed positions require staking with thin bamboo poles to stop them blowing over in high winds. With water lilies, leave them for three years after planting and then prune annually in early summer if they become invasive. This will prevent overgrowth and also encourage flowering. Some variegated plants, such as the zebra rush (*Scirpus tabernaemontani zebrinus*), tend to revert after a few years and any plain green leaves should be cut out as soon as they appear to help keep the plant strongly variegated.

Waterside plants on banks
1 *Remove the plant from its container and measure its roots. Handle carefully to avoid damaging the roots or reused. Enrich the topsoil with peat or organic matter and a handful of slow-release fertilizer.*

2 *Excavate a hole at least four times the size of the plant's root ball. Separate the topsoil so that it can be reused. Enrich the topsoil with peat or organic matter and a handful of slow-release fertilizer.*

3 *Center the plant in the hole, backfill with the enriched topsoil and firm it gently round the plant.*

4 *Use small stones and pebbles as a mulch to prevent the bank eroding above the plant.*

Planting a tree or shrub
First, strip away about 1sq m/11sq ft of turf. Excavate the topsoil and place it on a plastic sheet to one side, and then dig out the deeper soil to the same depth as the tree or bush in its pot. Keep this soil separate on its own sheet (1). Carefully remove the tree from its container and place it in the hole, with a stout tree stake well embedded in the bottom of the hole, off-center toward the side of any prevailing winds. Tie the tree temporarily to keep it fixed in position (2). Mix the topsoil with peat or compost and backfill, making sure that there are no gaps or air pockets around the roots. Firm the soil with your heel toward the sides of the hole to avoid damage to the tree roots. Apply two proper tree ties and then trim the stake to 2.5cm/1in below the lowest branch level (3).

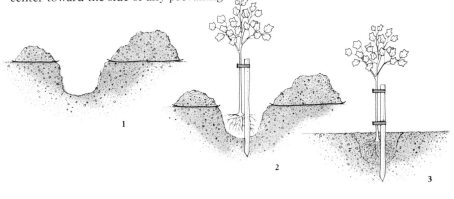

PLANNING FOR WILDLIFE

In both city and country surroundings, the variety of wildlife a water feature will support is amazing. And you can encourage local or passing wildlife to stop off at your pond or pool by providing a few home comforts: food is an obvious attraction as are nearby trees for birds, while smaller birds and mammals appreciate shallow edges where they can safely drink and bathe.

– FISH –

As well as the pleasure of seeing color and movement, fish serve an essential function by maintaining a healthy balance of gases in the water – as they take in oxygen they expel carbon dioxide, which is absorbed by water plants. These, in turn, photosynthesize and release oxygen back into the water. Fish will also eat aphids and mosquito larvae, and scavenger fish, such as the golden orfe (*Idus idus*), will clean up any edible material on the bottom.

Most species of fish are easy to look after and need only a few weeds for cover during hot weather and for protection in shallow ponds from predators and winter weather. You can feed them with any of the numerous brand-name preparations, available from all fish dealers, or with daphnia, boiled potatoes or even brown bread. Stop feeding fish in winter when their metabolic rate slows down and they basically live off their own body fats.

Koi carp are often referred to as the kings of the decorative fish and are bred for their impressive size – up to 1.2m/4ft in warm climates – and wonderful markings. Even kois half this size will require a depth of water of at least 90cm/36in, and the pond should have high sides (about 60cm/24in) to stop them jumping out onto the bank.

The popular goldfish (*Carassius auratus*) is a good, safe choice. Hardy and easy to keep, it grows to a length of about 13cm/5in and is bright gold or silver in color. Equally eyecatching is the golden rudd (*Scardinius erythrophthalmus*), which has red fins and tail and a golden-red overall color.

Try to include at least one scavenger fish in your pond. The green tench (*Tinca tinca*) is an impressive 45cm/18in long and is hardy, but because it keeps to the bottom it can only rarely be seen. A better choice is the golden orfe, which grows to about 30cm/12in and takes food from the surface as well.

Introducing fish to the pond

Do not attempt to introduce fish into your pond until it is well established – at least two weeks – to allow any chlorine in the water to evaporate. Concrete-lined pools need to be weathered for about three months, or sealed with a brand-name sealant, to prevent high levels of lime in the water.

The best time to buy and introduce fish is in the early spring, when they should be in good condition and the water will be warmer. The usual way of introducing fish to the pond is to float the plastic bag holding the fish on the surface of the water until the water in the

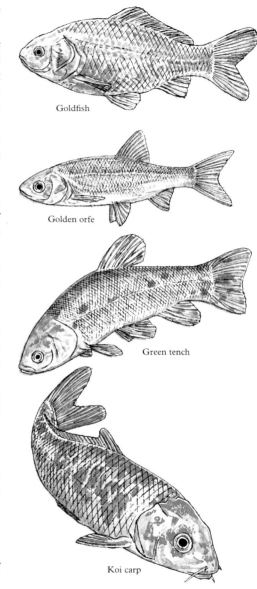

Goldfish

Golden orfe

Green tench

Koi carp

bag and that of the pond reach the same temperature. If you are not careful, you could leave the fish too exposed to heat and light, and unless the pond water is excessively hot or cold it is better simply to tip the fish directly into the water.

– WILDFOWL –

Larger ponds with substantial reed beds may attract a variety of wildfowl, including geese, ducks, moorhens and grebe. Unfortunately, these animals are prolific breeders and can easily overcrowd your site. As a general guide, allow no less than 10sq m/108sq ft per duck and twice this space for larger birds, such as geese.

Most birds will prefer 'islands' set out in the water, perhaps made of anchored wooden rafts, to sit on and plenty of straw to encourage nest building. Ducks like to dabble at the edge of water and so are not suited to a lined pond. Geese are hardy and aggressive, which makes them good 'watchdogs' but unfriendly pond companions. They are also voracious feeders and they will eat the plants.

Ducks and geese are both available in a wide selection of attractive breeds, and to stop them straying you will have to clip their flight feathers.

– SMALL ANIMALS AND INSECTS –

It will not take long for a pool or pond whatever its size and location, to become naturally populated. A waterfall or moving water feature will produce sufficient oxygen to support insect larvae of the mayfly or stonefly, which live under the stones and pebbles on the pond floor. Many other insect larvae are also aquatic. Caddis flies and hellgrammites live in well aerated water and, in fast-moving streams, these and mayfly larvae are prime food for brook trout. On the pond surface you should be able to see water striders and whirligig beetles and, beneath the surface, water boatmen and pea mussels. Keep a wary eye open for the great diving beetle, 3 to 3.5cm/1 to 1½in long and shiny black, which preys on tadpoles and small fish and should be netted and removed. And even the smallest pond will attract dragonflies.

In the reeds, it is not uncommon to find field mice nesting, also the harmless garter snake. Birds that are attracted to reed beds include both species of marsh wren as well as the swamp sparrow and red-winged blackbird.

There are many varieties of frogs, toads and newts depending on where you live. In Europe you should be able to find the common frog (*Rana temporaria*) and the marsh frog (*Rana ridibunda*); in North America the most common species is the attractively blotched leopard frog (*Rana pipiens*), a hardy specimen growing to a length of about 12cm/5in. The American bullfrog (*Rana catesbeiana*) is about 20cm/8in long and a little too large for most garden ponds. The smaller wood frog (*Rana sylvatica*), however, is only 7.5cm/3in long and common all over America. These frogs live in woodland, but need ponds in order to breed.

The common toad (*Bufo bufo*) and natterjack (*Bufo calamita*) are both hardy European natives, while the American toad (*Bufo americanus*) is particularly useful because it eats mosquitoes. Newts are becoming less common than they once were. In America the Japanese newt (*Cynops pyrrhogaster*) is popular in garden ponds, while in Europe the common newt (*Triturus vulgaris*) grows to about 6 to 8cm/2½ to 3in in length and the much larger great crested newt (*Triturus cristatus*) is 12 to 15cm/5 to 6in long.

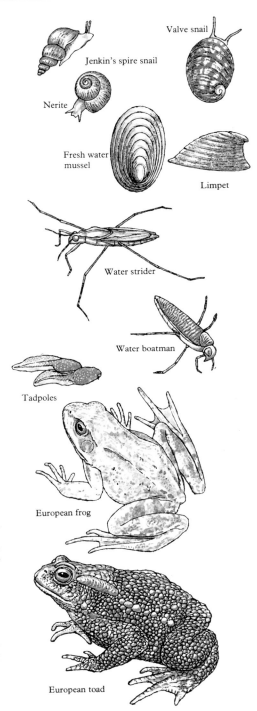

Valve snail

Jenkin's spire snail

Nerite

Fresh water mussel

Limpet

Water strider

Water boatman

Tadpoles

European frog

European toad

GENERAL CARE & UPKEEP

Provided they are well constructed in the first place and kept clean when in operation, most types of water feature are fairly easy to care for and maintain. With pools and ponds you should ensure that the correct level of water is always maintained, either by topping up during hot weather or draining off excess during the wet. This way you will avoid undue weathering of exposed sides or erosion of banks from flooding.

Cracks in concrete and tears in lining material can be repaired (see right), but it is a time-consuming business and obviously a problem best avoided. Properly mixed and treated concrete should not crack even under severe weather conditions.

Scummy water is a common problem with small ponds. A certain amount of algae is present in all water, but during long periods of high sunlight even the perfect balance of plants and fish is not enough and the water turns a livid green. In small, still-water ponds this problem can be overcome by the installation of a water filter (see p. 150). Larger stretches of water and natural ponds and pools fed by moving water are not usually troubled by this problem.

Water lilies can be prone to attack from lily beetles, which are best crushed between finger and thumb, and aphids, which can be swabbed off the leaves with damp cotton wadding. Spraying the leaves of all water plants at regular intervals with fresh water is a good idea, since it knocks any insects into the pond where the fish can eat them.

Provided your fish are not overfed and the water is well oxygenated, they should remain healthy. But if you do see one acting uncharacteristically or swimming lethargically with unusual swellings or blotches on its body, consult your local fish dealer and treat accordingly with one of the numerous brand-name medicines available.

– WINTER CARE –

Autumn and winter are not the best times of year to give your pond a thorough clean, since you will disturb all the plants and fish trying to acclimatize to the change of season – some plants even send down buds to the bottom where they lie until the weather becomes warmer. The best time for a good clean-up is in early spring when plant life is back in full swing and fish are actively feeding.

Unless sited near broad-leaved deciduous trees, ponds and pools need very little care during the winter months. An ugly buildup of leaves on the bottom will create unwelcome gases causing the water to go black and become smelly. If the pond is small enough it should be netted in early autumn before leaves start to fall; otherwise you will have to remove the leaves using a soft plastic scoop or rake. This is particularly important for concrete or plastic lined ponds, but large natural ponds and those with running water can be left to rid themselves of this type of vegetation.

To improve the appearance and as a precaution against disease, remove any

Repairing a butyl liner

1 *Make sure the torn liner is completely dry and clean and then prepare a butyl or bitumen mastic patch larger than the tear.*

2 *Both surfaces must be free from grease and dirt. Brush the torn liner with an appropriate waterproof latex solution or epoxy resin glue.*

3 *Apply latex solution or epoxy resin glue to the patch, making sure the surface is completely covered, and wait for the time recommended for the glue to become tacky.*

4 *Stick down the patch making sure there are no air pockets.*

5 *Paint over the total area with adhesive and wait at least six hours for it to dry before refilling the pool.*

rotting and dying vegetation from water and waterside plants after the first two or three frosts. Excess floating weeds that look dead can also be removed with a net or wire rake.

Fish will not now need feeding; just leave them to feed on natural food in the water, but they will basically be living off their own body fats built up during the summer months. Make sure they have plenty of cover in the form of rocks, ledges or deep areas where they can hide undisturbed.

Extreme winter weather

Pools deeper than about 60cm/24in are most unlikely to freeze completely and a regular flow of water from a fountain or waterfall is useful for keeping an area free from surface ice – providing it is not so cold that pumps and pipes freeze as well. If you are nervous about fish freezing, especially in shallow pools where they will not be able to retreat deep enough, and you cannot bring them indoors, install a small pool heater, available from large garden centers. Never break the ice with a hammer or other heavy object, since it only stuns and confuses the fish, and the freed area is likely to freeze over again even harder than before.

– SUMMER CARE –

Your main concern in summer will be to keep the water clean and well topped up, preferably from a rain barrel. Remove any leaves or dirt from the water and take care that no grass cuttings or rotting plant material fall into the pond. It is vitally important that no general garden fertilizers or chemicals get into the water where they could poison both plant and animal life.

If you see your fish coming to the surface to gasp for air during hot, dry weather, oxygen levels have dropped and you will need to drain between one-half and two-thirds of the water and replace it with fresh.

Extreme summer weather

Under drought conditions, it is better to keep the pond topped up from a slowly trickling hose rather than let the water level drop over a period of time before topping up. The slow, constant introduction of fresh water helps to maintain an even temperature in the water and more stable conditions for plants and fish. Bear in mind that evaporation is greater with a fountain or waterfall and these should be turned off when water is in short supply. If conditions are very severe, shade the water with mats or covers to reduce evaporation, and consider collecting water from a well or pump in case of rationing. In times of severe drought, transfer fish to a tank or water barrel and keep them in a shed or shaded greenhouse until they can be returned to the pond water.

– PUMP MAINTENANCE –

Modern submersible pumps are usually made from plastic, are self-lubricating and require very little maintenance. In dirty water or ponds with lots of water plants, pumps should be brought to the surface and the filter cleaned weekly. The pump itself should be stripped down and serviced at least once every year by a reputable dealer. The surge of water created when the pump is frequently turned on and off tends to clog the filter and it is better, for both pump and water, to keep it running continuously, even overnight. Water deeper than 60cm/24in

Repairing bank erosion
Erosion of unlined ponds or streams can be halted using well-treated lumber shoring driven firmly into the pond or stream bed. Batten the wood for extra strength and, using metal wire, tie this to substantial blocks of hardwood buried in the ground beyond the eroded area. Backfill the damaged portion of the bank.

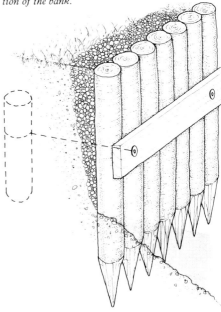

Preventing erosion
Various materials can be employed with shallow, unlined pond or stream edges. Large boulders (1) can be graduated back toward smaller stones and shingle along the slope of the bank. Or insert wooden ties (2) backed with shingle; with very shallow banks, line the area with stone or concrete paving slabs (3).

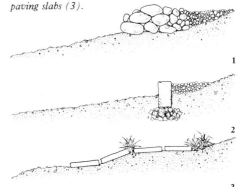

is unlikely to freeze and so submersible pumps can be left running in winter to operate a fountain or waterfall. In prolonged periods of freezing conditions, remove, clean, dry and store the pump in a shed or garage.

Surface pumps need a waterproof shelter or shed and regular annual maintenance by a qualified pump service company. All moving parts should be kept well greased and oiled to prevent clogging and seizing up, and, like submersible pumps, they operate with fewer problems if kept running continuously. In winter they should be drained and turned off.

You must be careful with surface pumps that you do not run them dry or forget to turn on the tap or release the valve that allows water from the pond to reach the pump. Nearly all models have a bleed screw that ensures there is water in the chamber before the pump is turned on, but these vary and it is best to check with your supplier. When restarting, turn on the tap from the pool and then check that the pump chamber is full. Whenever water depth allows, it is always better to use a submersible pump.

– MOVING WATER FEATURES –
Except under severe weather conditions, when snow and ice are likely to cover the ground for extended periods, moving water features such as fountains and waterfalls can be kept in operation. Running water does not freeze as easily as still water, and it can be useful for keeping pond water free from ice or preserving fountain basins and bird baths made of reconstituted stone or concrete, which are liable to crack in frost or ice. There is no need to keep concrete treated with an antifrost agent covered

with water, but it is advisable to keep the water running on very cold nights to stop the water pipes freezing. Regular cleaning should keep moving water features free from dirt and debris. In hard water areas, make sure narrow valves or nozzles do not become clogged with lime.

– SURFACES AND STRUCTURES –
Surrounding surfaces and structures, such as decks, bridges and pergolas, should be checked regularly to make sure they are safe and that all wood is sound. All exposed wood should be treated with preservative once a year and wooden surfaces underfoot scoured with a wire brush as often as is required to remove slippery algae or moss growth.

Other things to check for on a regular basis are rusting or missing screws and nails, and warped, twisted or weakened wooden sections, which should be cut out and replaced as soon as possible. Also check that any concrete reinforcing round the bottom of supporting lumber is not weathered or cracked and that exposed ironwork is not rusting. Any brackets supporting handrails or other safety features will also need regular inspection.

Paving, brickwork and tiles should need very little maintenance, except for sweeping clear of leaves, dirt and other debris, and occasional spot cleaning with a brand-name paving cleaner for stains and spills. Once a year, check that any pointing damaged by frost is raked out and replaced, otherwise the top surface material may work loose.

– SWIMMING POOLS AND HOT TUBS –
Because swimming pools and hot tubs are for personal use, they need to be scrupulously clean and conscientiously

Pool filters
If you have problems keeping your pool water clean and healthy – a common problem with small pools and ponds – it is certainly worth installing some form of water filter to keep the water circulating and well aerated. You have a choice between external filters, which can be connected to an existing pump and that recycle the water through a charcoal filter, and a filter enclosure, which comprises a neat sump in the bottom of the pool with a submersible pump filtering the water through stones or gravel. The filter enclosure system is really only suitable for very small pools, but both are inexpensive and easy to install.

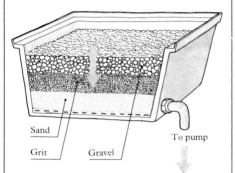

Sand

Grit   Gravel

To pump

Filter types
Commercial filters use trays of gravel, grit and sand to collect any dirt particles in a removable gauze filter pad (above). A simple homemade filter (below) can consist of a wire cage filled with gravel.

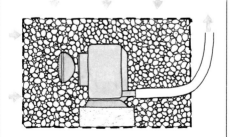

maintained. The time and expense involved in keeping such a feature in peak condition can be significant.

If you do not live in a climate that is hot all year round, you will have to heat your pool or tub and your supplier will advise you on a unit that is suitable for its size and shape. The only way to budget on cost is in your choice of fuel, which will depend on local availability, and in using solar covers, which are really effective only when there is prolonged sunshine. When a hot tub or pool is not in use, always keep it covered.

Water hygiene

Adequate filtration and proper sterilization are essential to pool and tub management. Filtration is usually achieved by high-speed sand filters through which the water is pumped. As the water passes through the sand, any dirt carried in the flow is trapped in the uppermost layers of sand and clean water is then returned to the pool or tub.

A finer degree of filtration is provided by the Diatomaceous Earth (DE) system. Here the water is passed through elements coated with a slurry made of the diatomaceous earth, which is composed of the siliceous shells of microscopic plants with extremely fine porosity.

Small swimming pools and spas are sometimes fitted with cartridge filters. These are not very efficient and are identical in principle to the type used to clean air and oil supplies in cars.

No filtration system is adequate by itself and proper sterilization of the water is necessary, too. This is achieved by one of several methods: chlorination, bromination, ozonation, electrolytic sterilization or Bacquacil treatment. The degree of treatment required depends on the weather, water temperature, bathing load and other factors clearly displayed on the product or accompanying literature. Water treated with these products must not be allowed to contaminate a planted pool or pond.

Chlorination is the best-known method of water sterilization; it has been thoroughly tried and tested over many years. Bromine comes from the same group of chemicals as chlorine and many of its properties are similar. Bromine, however, is thought to be less irritating to the eyes and faster acting than chlorine.

Ozone is used in conjunction with other disinfectants because, despite its excellent sterilizing qualities, it dissipates quickly leaving no residue to prevent cross-infection of bathers. On the plus side, ozone does not damage building materials, nor irritate eyes and skin.

The other methods of treating water are not generally used in domestic pools or tubs. There is, however, a new agent on the market from the chemical company ICI, known as Bacquacil, which, it is claimed, has overcome such side effects as toxicity, corrosion and irritation associated with more well-established agents. Until it has been tried and tested over a longer period it is difficult to say whether it will fulfil the claims being made.

Whichever system you use, chemicals are expensive, so use them correctly and take care to follow exactly the manufacturers' recommendations.

To shut down pools and hot tubs during winter, turn off pumps and filters and turn off the electricity and heating fuel supplies. Remove the top 5 to 7.5cm/2 to 3in of water to allow room for expansion in case the water freezes, give an extra 'shock' dose of chemicals and cover small pools and tubs securely.

Cutting back herbaceous plants
Herbaceous plants should be cut back to ground level using loppers, a sharp knife or pruners at the end of the season to allow for new spring growth.

Looking after Gunnera

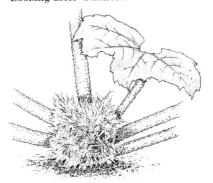

1 *In areas prone to severe frosts,* Gunnera *does need a little attention in autumn. Look carefully at the base of the plant and you will see its exposed crown.*

2 *Cut the thick leafy stems back right to the crown at the end of the summer season. Then carefully wrap the leaves over the crown to form a parcel to protect it during the cold months.*

SAFETY

◆

Although water is a wonderful garden asset, you must bear in mind that it is also potentially hazardous – especially if the garden is used by young children, the disabled or the elderly. Children are the ones mainly at risk and it is not advisable to install any type of pool or pond if you have children under five years old. It is perfectly safe, though, to install a bubble fountain (see p. 132) or wall-mounted spout, or you could even convert a small, formal pool into a sandpit or sunken play area until the children are a little older. One of the most effective safety precautions you can take if you have children is to teach them to swim.

– PLANNING FOR SAFETY –

All surfaces round or near a water feature such as a pond or pool should be made from nonslip materials and evenly laid on a well-constructed base (see pp. 138-40). In general, glazed tiles should be avoided as these can be slippery when wet. Instead, go for surface materials with a textured finish: these could include unglazed tiles, brick (treated with bleach to stop the growth of moss) and concrete. Brushing the surface of newly laid concrete will expose some of the aggregate, creating a very safe, nonslip finish. Use materials such as gravel, stones and cobbles only where there is little chance of anybody stumbling and falling, or to mark out 'no-go' areas for foot traffic to and from the pool. Loose material will need confining to stop it washing down into the water.

Fences and barriers

If you decide to install a large water feature, or take over a garden where one is already installed, and have a member of the family at risk from the water, it is a good idea to build a safety fence. Hot tubs and spas built flush with the ground may also need to be fenced off. A safety barrier need not be unattractive and could consist of a bamboo or wooden screen clothed with shrubs and flowering climbers. Make sure, however, that any gates giving access to the water's edge are firmly fixed to substantial uprights and fitted with childproof locks. The height of the barrier depends to a large extent on the age of the children you are trying to exclude – but about 1.2m/4ft should be considered the minimum to be an effective barrier.

Commercially produced safety fencing is another option and this is available from nearly all pool centers. This, however, is usually made from large sections of tubular metal and, as a result, is expensive to buy and install and probably too overpowering for the average garden setting.

Hot tubs, spas and small formal pools can be fitted with covers to shield completely the water's surface; larger expanses of water can be netted. The network need not cover the entire surface of the water; just the edges should be sufficient for safety.

Safety in the water

All swimming pools that are used by children or the elderly should be built with a shallow end and safety ledge running right round the pool area. Shallow steps leading gradually into the water are easier and safer to use than ladder-type stairs, which are better installed in

Handrails for wooden decking
A handrail is advisable for any area of raised decking, especially if it overhangs water. Supporting posts are usually bolted to the main structure using coach bolts and all wood should be well sanded and treated with preservative.

Handrails for extra security
Where you have young children likely to swing on the handrail, make sure that is is well bolted and rigid. As an added precaution, set the rail back from the edge of the deck surface so that if they do slip through, they do not fall into the water.

the deep end. When using bathing, ornamental or splash pools make sure that the water does not become polluted by broken glass. Use plastic cups and plates only anywhere near the water in preference to earthenware.

Lighting for safety

If the pool area is to be used at night it is especially important that any expanses of water are well lit and their limits clearly defined. This is particularly relevant to natural ponds and bog gardens where lush planting could disguise deep water areas. Even a few centimeters of surface water in a bog garden could be dangerous to a very young child. All access paths leading to these areas should also be well lit, as should any steps between different levels of the garden (see pp. 76-80 and pp. 142-3).

– PERSONAL SAFETY –

Building a pool or water feature can be strenuous and even dangerous if you are not properly equipped for the task. Thick gardening gloves will protect your hands from simple knocks and scratches as well as from allergic reactions to chemicals used in cement or to preserving materials. Eyes can be protected with plastic goggles, which should always be worn when using drills, chisels, grinders or sledgehammers. A hard hat is advisable if other building work is going on around you. Dungarees or overalls with knee pockets designed to accommodate foam wadding are excellent for jobs that require a lot of kneeling on hard surfaces and save wear and tear on trousers.

As an added safety precaution, do not wear rings or neck chains when working with machinery, and make sure that any loose clothing is well tucked in.

Saving your back

Lifting of heavy materials and pieces of equipment is unavoidable during some phases of construction work, and there are right and wrong ways of going about it. The first rule is to get help whenever you can and always to clear the route to your destination. It is important to get a good grip on the object you are lifting and then to keep your back as straight as possible and bend your knees, letting your legs take the strain. Keep your head up and the weight of the object as close to your body as possible when transporting it. When you want to put it down again, lower it slowly to the ground (keeping your back straight and bending your knees). Avoid dropping it with relief, since the sudden release can cause a whiplash action and perhaps damage your spine.

When using a wheelbarrow to move heavy loads, do not be tempted to overload it in order to save time – an overfull wheelbarrow is difficult to control over rough ground and you could well strain yourself trying to keep it balanced. With large objects, such as boulders and bags of sand or cement, you should tip the wheelbarrow on its side and roll the object into it. Pulling the wheelbarrow upright is easier than lifting the object from the ground. You will find that a pneumatic tire makes heavy loads much easier to push. An alternative method of moving heavy loads is to use a series of wooden rollers and a stout rope. Pull the object along, moving the back roller up to the front as you progress. If this proves too difficult over very uneven ground, then roll the object onto a piece of old carpet or heavy-duty sacking and drag it instead. Never put your back at risk if you are feeling cold or tired.

Lifting heavy objects
To avoid damaging your back when lifting heavy objects, always bend from the knees and never the spine. Keep your back straight and your head up, letting your legs take the strain, and keep the weight close to your body. Never drop a weight suddenly; bend your knees and release the object carefully onto the ground.

Using a wheelbarrow
With large objects, tip the wheelbarrow on its side and roll the object into it. Righting the wheelbarrow from this position will be less difficult than lifting the object from the ground and placing it in. An overloaded wheelbarrow will be difficult and strenuous to control, especially over rough ground.

PESTS & DISEASES

Water plants are usually free of disease and are less trouble to look after than ordinary garden plants. There is, however, one disease that attacks water lilies in particular – *cercosporae*. This is a fungal disease, which first shows as spots on the lily leaves. The leaves then tend to become dry and crumpled and this obviously affects the growth of the plants. The incidence of *cercosporae* is relatively uncommon and a dusting of Bordeaux mixture will sometimes cure the disorder if it is not too advanced. The surest method of preventing its spread is, however, to remove the affected leaves and, if the plant does not recover, to remove the whole plant from the water and destroy it.

Pests in the water are certainly more of a problem and, depending on the size and extent of your pond or pool, can be difficult to deal with. The larvae of the caddis fly feeds on water lilies and often attacks the flower buds. The best method of dealing with this problem is by introducing fish into the water, since the larvae make excellent natural fish food. The distribution of the caddis fly is, thankfully, sporadic, and you will most likely not be worried by it.

Another pest to look out for in the water garden is the water lily beetle. This beetle attacks and eats the leaves of the water lily and, again, it is best kept under control by the presence of fish in the water. The caterpillar of the brown China marks moth also feeds on the leaves of water lilies and hides by constructing oval cases out of pieces of leaf tissue. The only effective way of dealing with it is regularly to inspect the leaves of your plants and remove by hand any caterpillars you find.

Chemical treatment

The use of chemicals to control pests and diseases in the pond should be discouraged, since they are a source of water pollution, and fish, in particular, are very susceptible to most chemical treatments. Where aphids are a problem, the best method of treatment is to remove affected leaves and then burn them. Aphids lay their eggs on the leaves of plants and the emerging larvae will then commence to feed on them. Any eggs swabbed off the leaves will be eaten readily by the fish.

Waterside plants

Plants growing around the margins of a water feature are very likely to be attacked by slugs and snails, which love the damp, moist conditions to be found there. A popular method of dealing with this is to use one of the many brand-name slug and snail killers on the market. If, however, you have pets or you are worried about the effect these chemical killers have on birds, then there are completely safe 'natural' alternatives. You can, for example, place half a grapefruit or orange on the ground, cut side downward, and then allow the slugs and snails to crawl underneath and begin to feed. Then, once a day, you can collect and kill them. Another method is to sink a small container of beer flush with the ground. This attracts the slugs and snails, which fall into the liquid and drown.

AILMENT	TYPES OF FISH AFFECTED	HOW TO RECOGNIZE	TREATMENT
Fin congestion and rot	Long-finned goldfish and shubunkins	Red streaking of the caudal fin, fish remain stationary yet move their bodies from side to side.	Increase temperature of the water, possible antibiotic or phenoxethol.
Fungus	Most ornamental fish	Cotton woollike appearance.	A salt solution made up using 5 grams of salt per liter of water. Fish should be immersed on a daily basis up to 30 minutes at a time.
Anchor worm or fish lice	Most common to ornamental fish, goldfish, koi carp	Anchor worms attach themselves to the skin of the fish; fish lice are smaller and also attach themselves to the fish.	Remove fish from pond, remove lice or anchor worms with tweezers, treat with iodine or salt water after removing. Alternatively, treat with concentrated potassium permanganate solution applied with a small brush.
White spot	Most pond fish	White dots that cover the skins and fins of fish.	Remove all fish from pond that show this parasite, and place in running water in aquarium. Treat with $2\frac{1}{2}\%$ solution of mecurichrome in over 10 liters of water.
Red pest	Most ornamental fish	Blood vessels on belly become engorged and appear very red.	Usually prevalent where fish are overcrowded. Thin out fish, increase water circulation.
Body rot	Goldfish and koi carp	An ulcer on the body.	Antibiotic, not usually effective.

Fish

Fish are of a great benefit to the water gardener, both for the pleasure they give when observed darting around in the water, and because they help to control many harmful or annoying insect populations. Mosquitoes, for example, can breed only in still water, such as is found in many garden ponds and pools. In most cases, goldfish, koi carp or golden orfe, three very popular pond fish, will eat either the mosquito eggs or larvae before they have the chance to develop into flying, biting pests.

Unless the pond is kept clean (see pp. 148-51), fish can become susceptible to a number of different diseases. In the chart (see left), some of the more common disease symptoms are given, along with recommended treatments. As a general rule, however, as soon as you see a fish behaving in an uncharacteristic way, or showing unusual markings, color changes, or body swellings, it should be netted and kept in isolation until you have determined that it is not contagious.

The majority of pond owners will have no option other than to leave their fish outside over winter. There, the fish will settle near the bottom of the pond and remain dormant. Should there be, however, a period when the surface of the water is completely covered by ice, you should place a pool heater, available from specialist suppliers, in the water. The heater will melt at least a small area of the ice, and so allow the escape of potentially lethal gases produced by decaying vegetation and fish waste products.

In spring, you should start normal feeding of your fish as soon as they become active. Overfed fish are more prone to disease than those that are fed a healthy, well-balanced diet.

GLOSSARY

A

Acid In gardening, a term applied to soils with a pH lower than 7.0.

Aeration The loosening of soil by various mechanical means to allow a free passage of air.

Aggregate Small pieces of broken stone, coarse gravel, or other rocklike materials used in the making of concrete.

Algae Simple unicellular organisms, which cause pool and pond water to look green. These organisms multiply rapidly in conditions of high temperature and high natural light levels.

Alkaline In gardening, a term applied to soils with a pH higher than 7.0, normally with a comparatively high lime content.

Annual A plant that germinates, grows, flowers, seeds and dies within the space of 12 months.

Aquatic Term applied to a plant of any genera capable of living with its roots, stems and sometimes its leaves submerged in water.

B

Backfilling Adding soil, rubble, gravel, etc. to fill an area to the required level.

Ball valve Automatic device to control the water level of a pond or pool. A lightweight ball floats on the surface of the water. When the water level drops, a rod attached to the ball releases a valve, which allows water to flow in. As the ball rises, the rod progressively closes the valve.

Bearers Load-bearing lumbers used in the construction of wooden decks.

Beveled Anything having a sloped edge. Lumber on the exposed edges of a wooden deck, for example, could be beveled for a neat finish.

Biennial A plant that germinates, grows, flowers, seeds and dies within a period of two years.

Bog Damp area of poorly drained acid soil that remains waterlogged under normal conditions.

Bog garden Area of poorly drained ground resembling bog conditions and planted with bog and waterside plants.

Bog plants Plants that will tolerate the continually wet conditions found in a bog.

Bubble fountain Fountain effect producing a low bubble of water forced up by a pump concealed in an underground reservoir of water.

Bulb A storage organ with fleshy scales or a swollen leaf base containing food for a resting period.

Butyl A waterproof, rubberlike material used to line certain types of pools and ponds.

C

Calcareous A term applied to soil impregnated with lime.

Chalk Calcium carbonate, chemically identical to limestone. Chalk is used as a hydrated lime to counteract a high acid content in soils; a chalk soil has a high pH.

Chicken wire A lightweight wire mesh used as a strengthening material with poured concrete.

Chlorine A chemical used to sterilize water.

Clay A term applied to a soil mixture of very fine sand and alumina, which is moisture-retentive, heavy and sticky but usually fertile if treated.

Clay puddling A technique used for sealing and waterproofing the sides and base of large natural ponds by 'puddling', or working, the natural or added clay by hand, foot, or machine.

Compost The product of rotten vegetable matter.

Conduit A channel or pipe, often made of plastic, used as a protective cover for electric cables, etc.

Cordate A leaf with two rounded lobes at its base.

Corm A storage organ comprising a thickened underground stem.

Crown The top of the rootstock from which new shoots grow.

Cultivar Cultivated variety either bred purposely or developing spontaneously, but incapable of exact reproduction by seeds.

Culvert Channel or conduit for carrying water, electric cables, etc. Large, concrete-made culverts can be used to support the span of a bridge.

D

Deciduous A term applied to a plant or tree that drops its leaves in winter.

Deck A low wooden platform structure usually supported by bearers.

Dormant A condition of inactivity in plants usually occasioned by low temperatures.

Dowel A headless pin made of wood or metal used for fastening.

DPC Stands for damp-proof course. An impervious material used near the base of a building to stop damp rising up the structure.

Dump-mounted backhoe Small earth-moving machine used in the excavation of ponds and pools.

E

Erosion The gradual wearing away and destruction of soil, etc., due to the effects of water and wind.

Evergreen A term applied to a plant or tree that drops and replaces its leaves gradually throughout the year, so that its branches are never bare.

Exotic A plant not indigenous to the country in which it is growing, and which is not able to naturalize.

F

Filter A device for removing suspended particles from the water.

Form Lumber used to construct a temporary support for wet concrete. It is sometimes known as formwork.

Friable Soil with a high organic content that crumbles easily.

Fungicide A substance used for destroying fungal diseases, usually based on copper or sulfur.

G

Genus Part of the botanical classification of plants. It identifies a group of allied species (plural: genera).

Gravel A mixture of rock fragments and small pebbles that is coarser than sand.

Ground cover Thickly growing low shrubs or herbaceous plants that closely cover the soil which supports them. They are often used to suppress the growth of weeds.

H

Habit The general appearance or manner or growth of a plant: e.g., upright, weeping, creeping, etc.

Half-hardy A term applied to a plant that needs protection in winter if there is a chance of frosts.

Hardwood A resilient timber from deciduous trees. It is very resistant to rotting and, although expensive, is excellent for wooden decks, etc.

Hardy A plant that is capable of surviving all year round in cold climates.

Herbaceous A term applied to a plant with a soft or sappy, instead of woody, growth.

Hot tub A large wooden barrel fitted with seats and connected to a pump, filter, heater and bubble equipment for water massage. It is usually installed above ground.

Humus Decayed organic matter. It is used as a soil conditioner rather than as a fertilizer.

Hybrid The product of a cross between plants of different species. It is often indicated by a cross (×) between two other plant names.

IJ

Inorganic A fertilizer or any chemical compound without carbon.

Insecticide A chemical substance used to kill harmful insects. A wide variety of products is available, either in liquid or powder form. Very selective insecticides are now commonly available and all should be used according to the accompanying instructions.

Joists Parallel boards used to provide support for planks, such as in a wooden deck.

L

Landscape architect A garden designer who tries to imitate the natural landscape.

Landscaping The design of a garden or plot in imitation of the natural landscape. It also applies to the integrating of a feature into an already established garden design.

Larva The growth stage of some animals between egg and adult.

Leaf mold The part-decayed leaves that have reached the flaky, brown stage. It looks a little like coarse peat.

Level A glass tube of spirit used to check that a horizontal or vertical surface is level.

Loam Rotted turf; normally a soil mixture of sand, clay and humus.

M

Marsh Land that is permanently submerged beneath a few centimeters of water.

Masonry bolt An expanding rawlbolt used for very strong fitting of wood, for example, into brickwork and stonework.

Mulch Any decayed or part-decayed organic matter that is spread around the base of plants. It is useful for preventing excessive evaporation of moisture from the soil and also helps to feed the plants. If weed suppression only is required, then inorganic material, such as gravel, can be used as a mulch.

NO

Native A term applied to a plant that is indigenous to a locality or country.

Naturalize The process of growing plants under conditions that are as nearly natural as is possible. Naturalized plants are those that were originally imported but have subsequently reseeded themselves into the wild.

Nontoxic A substance that is not poisonous.

Nursery bed A separate soil bed used for seeding and growing young plants until they are mature enough to be planted out in their permanent positions.

Oxygenating A term applied to a plant that grows in or under water and which produces oxygen. Particularly useful in ponds and pools.

P

Palmate A term applied to a leaf shaped like a hand.

Panicle A flower cluster of several separate branches, each carrying numerous stalked flowers.

Peat Acidic, part-decayed organic matter used as a planting medium. Moss peat comes from mainly decomposed sphagnum moss, whereas sedge peat comes from the roots and leaves of sedges.

Peltate A term applied to a shield-shaped leaf with a central stalk.

Perennial Any plant that lives and flowers for a number of years.

Pergola A trellis structure, usually made of wood, useful for climbing plants and creating shade, arbors and arches.

Photosynthesis The process whereby energy is absorbed by chlorophyll from sunlight.

pH A measure of the acidity or alkalinity of soil.

Pier A columnar support for an arch or a span of a bridge or jetty.

Pile driver A machine for driving posts into the ground.

Pinnate A term applied to a featherlike leaf having several leaflets on each side of a common stalk.

Preservative A chemical substance used to treat wood to prevent rot and decay.

Propagation The increase of plant stocks either by seed or by layering, cutting, division or grafting.

Pump A device for raising or moving water.

R

Raceme An unbranched inflorescence with flowers carried on equal-length stalks.

RCCB Stands for residual current circuit breaker; a cut-out device used to detect any irregularity in an electric current.

Rhizome An underground stem that usually grows horizontally, producing shoots some distance from the parent.

Root ball A cluster of roots embedded in soil.

S

Saggitate A term applied to an arrow-shaped leaf with two lobes projecting backward, giving it the appearance of an arrow head.

Shingle Small round pebbles sometimes used as a surface material for paths, etc.

Shrub A multi-stemmed woody plant smaller than a tree.

Softwood A soft timber from coniferous trees, susceptible to decay.

Spa A preformed bath or tub with built-in whirlpool action for underwater massage. It is usually installed flush with the ground.

Space tumbler A device for determining the angle of a slope in construction.

Species A group of plants that resemble each other, breed together and maintain the same constant distinctive character.

Specimen plant A tree or shrub grown so that it is prominent and can be seen from many different angles.

Stagnant Water that is stale and sluggish, usually lacking in oxygen.

Stake A straight length of cane, or anything similar, used to support top-heavy plants or shrubs. Stakes are often used when planting trees and can be removed when the roots are established.

Straightedge A straight length of unwarped board used to maintain a straight line. Often used in garden construction.

Subsoil A layer of organically dead soil found beneath the surface, or top, soil.

T

Taproot A straight root, thicker at its top than at its bottom, from which subsidiary roots grow.

Tender A plant that is not capable of withstanding frosts and cold, damp conditions.

Topsoil The top layer of soil comprising viable, organic matter.

T-piece A T-shaped connection used to join three different pipes.

V

Variegation Usually white or light yellow markings on otherwise green leaves. This can arise from a mutation and then be bred true, or it can result from a mineral deficiency or a virus.

Variety A group of plants within a species; any plant with distinctive characteristics but not worthy of a specific rank.

W

Watercourse A formal waterway, with straight, parallel sides.

Water meadow A frequently flooded, low-lying area of ground usually comprising rough grass and supporting a variety of wild plants and flowers.

Waterside plant A term applied to a plant that grows in shallow water at the margin, or edge, of a pool or pond. Also known as emergent plants.

Waterside shelf A shallow shelf built into the side of a pool where waterside plants can be stood in baskets or planted.

Water table The level under the ground to which water naturally drains. This varies from locality to locality depending on the composition of the underlying rock.

Weir A dam built across a stream or river designed to raise the water level upstream.

Well-light Outdoor lighting equipment set flush with the ground and covered by a specially toughened glass safety lens.

Wild garden A type of planting design that endeavors to imitate a naturally occurring arrangement of shrubs, trees, and flowers. Assuming that no one plant becomes too invasive, this informal style of garden does not require much maintenance.

PLANTS FOR SPECIFIC SITUATIONS

The following comprise a selection of those plants that require, or do well in, specific conditions, such as full sun or full shade. Also listed are dwarf varieties, plants for added height and breadth and those useful for ground or water cover. To help you to devise the best possible planting design, plant flowering seasons and flower color have been separately listed.

Key w = waterside plant; s = shrub; a = aquatic; wl = water lily; t = tree.

Shade-tolerant plants

Acer griseum (t)
Adiantum aethiopicum (w)
Arundinaria japonica (s)
Azalea (s)
Betula occidentalis (t)
Betula pendula (t)
Brunnera macrophylla (w)
Cornus alba 'Sibirica' (s)
Cornus kousa (s)
Geum rivale (w)
Hosta spp. (w)
Juncus effusus 'Spiralis' (w)
Lgularia spp. (w)
Lysimachia punctata (w)
Matteuccia struthiopteris (w)
Onoclea sensibilis (w)
Osmunda regalis (w)
Petasites (w)
Phyllitis scolopendrium (w)
Phyllostachys nigra (s)
Polygonum bistorta (w)
Rhododendron spp. (s)
Rodgersia (w)

Sun-tolerant plants

Arundo donax (w)
Butomus umbellatus (w)
Callistemon viminalis (s)
Cyperus alternifolius (t)
Hemerocallis (w)
Iris kaempferi (w)
Metesequoia glyptostroboides (t)
Orontium aquaticum (a)
Peltiphyllum peltatum (w)
Phormium (s)
Salix alba 'Britzensis' (t)
Salix chrysocoma (t)
Salix matsudana 'Tortuosa' (t)
Sorbaria aitchisonii (s)
Taxodium distichum (t)

Dwarf varieties

Acorus gramineus pusillus (w)
Hydrocharis morsus-ranae (a)
Lemna minor (a)
Nymphaea 'Escarboucle' (wl)
Nymphaea pygmaea alba (wl)
Typha minima (w)

Plants to add height

Arundo donax (w)
Arundinaria japonica (s)
Azalea (s)
Cardiocrinum giganteum (w)
Cornus alba 'Sibirica' (s)
Cyperus longus (w)
Cyperus papyrus (w)
Dicksonia antarctica (w)
Gunnera manicata (w)
Heracleum mantegazzianum (w)
Juncus effusus 'Spiralis' (w)
Kalmia latifolia (s)
Miscanthus sacchariflorus (w)
Miscanthus sinensis zebrinus (w)
Osmunda regalis (w)
Phormium (s)
Phyllostachys aureosulcata (s)
Phyllostachys nigra (s)
Rhododendron spp. (s)
Sasa palmata (s)
Scirpus lacustris (w)
Sorbaria aitchisonii (s)

Plants to add breadth

Brunnera macrophylla (w)
Cardiocrinum giganteum (w)
Eupatorium purpureum (w)
Gunnera manicata (w)
Ligularia spp. (w)
Lysichitum americanum (w)
Peltiphyllum peltatum (w)
Petasites (w)
Rheum palmatum (w)
Rhododendron spp. (s)
Rodgersia (w)
Sasa palmata (s)
Stratiotes aloides (a)
Zantedeschia aethiopica (w)

Plants to cover ground or water

Astilbe chinensis 'Pumila' (w)
Calla palustris (w)
Geum rivale (w)
Hosta spp. (w)
Lemna minor (a)
Lysimachia nummularia (w)
Mimulus guttatus (a)
Petasites japonicus (w)
Ranunculus aquatilis (a)

Spring-flowering plants

Aponogeton distachyus (w) yellow
Azalea spp. (s) various
Caltha palustris (w) yellow
Geum rivale (w) red-brown
Lysichitum americanum (w) yellow
Orontium aquaticum (a) white/gold
Primula pulverulenta (w) deep red
Ranunculus aquatilis (a) white

Summer-flowering plants

Artemisia lactiflora (w) cream
Astilbe (w) various
Butomus umbellatus (a) pink
Filipendula 'Plena' (w) white
Hemerocallis flava (w) yellow
Heracleum mantegazzianum (w) white
Hosta spp. (w) lilac
Iris spp. (w) various
Iris kaempferi (a) various
Iris laevigata (a) blue
Iris pseudacorus (a) yellow
Liriodendron tulipifera (t) yellow-green
Lythrum salicaria (w) red-purple
Mimulus (w) red, pink, purple
Nymphaea alba (wl) white
Nymphaea 'Gladstoniana' (wl) white
Nymphaea 'Laydekeri Fulgens' (wl) red
Nymphaea × *marliacea* 'Chromatella' (wl) yellow
Nymphaea odorata (wl) white/pink
Nymphaea 'Sunrise' (wl) yellow
Pontederia cordata (a) blue
Rheum palmatum 'Purpureum' (w) pink
Rhododendron spp. (s) various
Sagittaria sagittifolia (a) white
Zantedeschia aethiopica (w) white

Autumn-flowering plants

Aponogeton distachyus (a) white
Eupatorium (w) purple
Ligularia clivorum (w) orange
Lysimachia punctata (w) yellow
Mentha aquatica (a) blue
Pontederia cordata (w) blue
Rodgersia pinnata (w) various

INDEX

ACKNOWLEDGMENTS

Authors' acknowledgments

We would like to thank all those who have given advice and information and helped with the preparation of this book, including:
Keith Andrae at Surbiton Aquaria Co Ltd; Maurice Brill at Lighting Workshop; Graham Burgess; John Duane; David Fletcher at Hot Tubs; Bruce Harding at Guncast Ltd; Brian and Frances Huxham; John Kelly; David Palliser; Hannah Peschar Sculpture Gallery; William Pye and Henk Weijers.
We would specially like to thank Andrew Butcher, who produced much of the technical material throughout the book.

Publishers' acknowledgments

The publishers would like to thank the following individuals for their help in preparing this book. For allowing their gardens to be photographed: Mr and Mrs Irvine, Mr and Mrs McColl and Michael and Edith Paul. For their help with the design of the book: Polly Dawes and Anne Wilson. Thanks also go to Joanna Chisholm and Hal Bruce for their help with the preparation of the American edition, to Cathy Gill for the index and to Amanda Malpass for office services. Special thanks go to Sally Launder for her botanical illustrations.

Project editor Jonathan Hilton
Designer Steven Wooster

Text editor Alison Freegard
Picture researcher Anne Fraser

Typesetting
Chambers Wallace Ltd, London

Reproduction
Universal Colour Scanning Ltd, Hong Kong

Photographers

Peter Baistow 1, 8 (l), 10, 12 (l), 65
Michael Boys Syndication 17, 54
Karl-Dietrich Bühler 74
Geoff Dann 94 (r), 111 (r), 120 (r)
Henk Dijkman 25, 37, 38, 44, 45, 87, 98, 99, 111 (t)
Inge Espen-Hansen 16, 19 (b), 22 (t), 56, 110 (t), 113 (tl), 119
John Glover 4, 97
Jacqui Hurst 9, 19 (t), 95
Jerry Harpur 57, 59, 61, 64 (Compton Acres, Poole), 118 (Arley Hall, Cheshire)
Practical Householder 18
Gary Rogers 8 (r), 11, 20, 55, 75
Harry Smith Horticultural Photographic Collection 112, 113 (tr and bl)
Ron Sutherland 2, 12 (r), 13-14, 22 (b), 23-4, 27-31, 33-5, 40-2, 46-52, 62, 63 (b), 66-7, 69-73, 76-7, 79-80, 83-4, 88-90, 92, 94 (l), 105, 110 (b), 111 (bl), 120 (l), back cover
Elizabeth Whiting & Associates/ Karl-Dietrich Bühler front cover, 21, 96

Illustrators

David Ashby 75, 76, 85, 86, 89, 91, 124, 125 (t), 146, 147
Will Giles 48, 82, 125 (b), 126-45, 148-53 148-53
Sally Launder 7, 10, 15, 53, 58, 60, 62, 64, 68, 71, 72, 81, 92, 93, 100-101, 103, 104, 106-107, 108, 109, 114-15, 116-17, 123
Paul Stubbs 26, 32, 34, 36, 39, 43, 47, 50, 78

Garden designers

Michael Branch 61
Dick Huigens 74, 96
Brian Huxham (Prestige Pools) 13, 34, 35, 51, 52, 72, 88, 90 (r)
Anthony Paul 12 (r), 22 (b), 27-31, 33, 40-2, 46-9, 66-7, 69 (t), 70-1, 76-7, 79-80, 83, 84 (r), 89, 92, 111 (bl)
John Perkins 18
Alex Rota 57
Henk Weijers cover, 21, 25, 37, 38, 44-5, 87, 98-9, 111 (t)
Western Red Tub Co Pty Ltd 84 (l)
John Whittington 73

Sculptors

Michael Marriott 67 (bridge builder – Martin Cundell)
William Pye 63 (both)
Andrew Wallace 62

KEY r = right; l = left; t = top; b = bottom; tl = top left; tr = top right; bl = bottom left